GRENVILLE DAVEY

KATHARINA FRITSCH

ROBERT GOBER

JEFF KOONS

ANNETTE LEMIEUX

JUAN MUÑOZ

JULIAN OPIE

HAIM STEINBACH

OBJECTIVES:
THE NEW SCULPTURE

Organized by

Paul Schimmel

Chief Curator

Newport Harbor

Art Museum

ESSAYISTS

Kenneth Baker

Lucinda Barnes

Rosetta Brooks

Dan Cameron

Lynne Cooke

Jean-Pierre Dubost

Paul Schimmel

Peter Schjeldahl

Elisabeth Sussman

Stephan Schmidt-Wulffen

Copublished by

Newport Harbor

Art Museum

Newport Beach

California and

Rizzoli NEW YORK

The exhibition *OBJECTives: The New Sculpture*
was made possible by a generous gift from The Irvine Company, Newport
Beach, California. Additional funding was provided by the National Endowment for the Arts, a federal agency.

This book has been copublished by the Newport Harbor Art Museum and
Rizzoli International Publications, Inc., 300 Park Avenue South, New York,
NY 10010.

©Copyright 1990,
Newport Harbor Art Museum
850 San Clemente Drive
Newport Beach, California 92660
(714) 759-1122

Edited by Sue Henger
Designed by David Tanimoto
Printed and bound in Japan

LIBRARY OF CONGRESS CATALOGING-IN-PUBLICATION DATA
Objectives: the new sculpture / organized by Paul Schimmel ;
essayists, Dan Cameron, Paul Schimmel, Kenneth Baker. . . [et al].
        p. cm.
    Includes bibliographical references.
    ISBN 0-8478-1207-3 (Rizzoli). — ISBN 0-917493-15-X
    1. Sculpture, Modern—20th century—Themes, motives.
I. Schimmel, Paul.   II. Cameron, Dan.   III. Baker, Kenneth, 1946-
NB198.025   1990
730′.9′04807479496-dc20   89-48388
                                                                        CIP

COVER ILLUSTRATIONS, TOP TO BOTTOM:
Grenville Davey
    Grey Seal, 1987 (p. 35)
Robert Gober
    Installation at Paula Cooper Gallery, 1989
    Wedding Gown, 1989; *Hanging Man/*
    Sleeping Man (wallpaper), 1989 (p. 81)
Annette Lemieux
    Showing Ones Colors, 1986 (p. 101)
Katharina Fritsch
    Ghost and Pool of Blood, 1988 (p. 64 and 65)
Juan Muñoz
    The Waste Land, 1986 (p. 129)
Jeff Koons
    Flowers, 1986 (p. 89)
Julian Opie
    Night Light 22/3333CY, 1989
    (no plate in catalog)
Haim Steinbach
    sweetest taboo, 1987 (p. 155)

SPONSOR'S STATEMENT

With *OBJECTives: The New Sculpture*, the Newport
Harbor Art Museum builds on its tradition of
presenting thematic explorations of international
trends in contemporary art. The exhibition brings
American and European artists together in an
ambitious, in-depth examination of the changing
role of the object in recent sculpture.

The Irvine Company applauds the Museum for
undertaking this significant exhibition. We feel most
fortunate to be able to support and share with
others such an exciting scholarly venture.

Donald Bren
Chairman of the Board
🌀 THE IRVINE COMPANY

CONTENTS

LENDERS TO THE EXHIBITION

Eli and Edythe L. Broad, Santa Monica

Leo Castelli, New York

Robert and Honey Dootson, Seattle

Studio Guenzani, Milan

Ydessa Hendeles, Courtesy Ydessa Hendeles Foundation, Toronto

Ronnie and Samuel Heyman, New York

Anne and William Hokin, Chicago

Jeff Koons, New York

Alice and Marvin Kosmin, New York, Courtesy Josh Baer Gallery, New York

Barbara and Richard S. Lane, New York

Annette Lemieux, Boston

Lisson Gallery, London

Andrew Ong, New York

Private Collection, Laguna Beach

Private Collection, Laguna Beach, Courtesy of Sonnabend Gallery,

Private Collection, New York

Private Collection, Switzerland

Mera and Donald Rubell, New York

Saatchi Collection, London

Sonnabend Gallery, New York

Sonnabend Gallery, New York, and Jay Gorney Modern Art, New York

FOREWORD

OBJECTives: The New Sculpture, a survey of recent international sculpture, continues the Museum's program of tracking contemporary trends in art. In keeping with our tradition of featuring a small, select group of artists in order to give a detailed view of their work—a tradition exemplified by three past exhibitions exploring abstract expressionism and by participation in shows such as *British Sculpture Since 1965—OBJECTives* presents the recent work of eight sculptors in individual, self-contained installations. The artists, Grenville Davey, Katharina Fritsch, Robert Gober, Jeff Koons, Annette Lemieux, Juan Muñoz, Julian Opie, and Haim Steinbach share an innovative spirit that has highlighted them as among the most significant sculptors to emerge on the international scene in the 1980s.

OBJECTives marks the final exhibition to be organized by Chief Curator Paul Schimmel during his nearly nine-year tenure at the Museum. We applaud the man whose imaginative curatorship has led the Museum to international renown.

The exhibition has come to fruition through a generous gift from The Irvine Company, its seventh annual contribution in support of a major exhibition at the Museum. The Museum is also honored to have been awarded two National Endowment for the Arts grants for this project, one for research and a second for implementation. We are pleased to have the cooperation of Rizzoli International Publications in the copublication of the exhibition catalog, which features illustrated essays on the work of the eight artists and places their work in the broad context of postmodern art.

I would like especially to thank the Board of Trustees for their support of the exhibition program in general and this complex project in particular.

Thomas H. Nielsen
President, Board of Trustees

ACKNOWLEDGMENTS

Six years years ago, the Newport Harbor Art Museum was in the early stages of researching an exhibition entitled "Sign, Symbol, Object, Metaphor." It was apparent then, as it is even more so today, that a generation of young artists was moving rapidly away from the neofigurative tendencies that characterized so much of the painting of the early 1980s toward an art that, in many respects, is a continuation of the minimalist concerns of the sixties and the conceptual tendencies of the seventies. That germ of an exhibition has become *OBJECTives: The New Sculpture*, an exhibition that explores major sculptural tendencies in both America and Europe in the last five years of the 1980s.

OBJECTives has involved the creative involvement of the participating artists, Grenville Davey, Katharina Fritsch, Robert Gober, Jeff Koons, Annette Lemieux, Juan Muñoz, Julian Opie, and Haim Steinbach, who have either created or directly participated in the selection of discrete bodies of works and/or room-size installations for the exhibition. Each artist's willingness to participate in *OBJECTives* is deeply appreciated, for without their commitment this exhibition would not have been possible.

In addition to loans from the artists, works have been lent by more than twenty individual collectors and galleries to whom our gratitude is extended. Both the fragility of the sculpture and the value associated with the extraordinary success of many of these artists make it all the more generous for individuals, foundations and galleries to commit works. The participation of these lenders is greatly appreciated: Eli and Edythe L. Broad; Michele DeAngelus of The Eli Broad Family Foundation; Leo Castelli; Robert and Honey Dootson; Jay Gorney; Claudio Guenzani of Studio Guenzani; Ydessa Hendeles; Sheila Lawson of the Ydessa Hendeles Art Foundation; Ronnie and Samuel Heyman; Anne and William Hokin; Jeff Koons; Ann Rickey, assistant to Jeff Koons; Alice and Marvin Kosmin; Barbara and Richard S. Lane; Annette Lemieux; Elisabeth McCrae and Nicholas Logsdail of Lisson Gallery, London; Andrew Ong; Mera and Donald Rubell; Charles Saatchi; Julia Ernst of the Saatchi Collection; and Antonio Homem, Stefano Basilico, and Nick Sheidy of the Sonnabend Gallery.

I would like to express my appreciation to a number of individuals who have in some substantial way helped in the conceptual development of this exhibition. Tom Heller, a former assistant curator at the Newport Harbor Art Museum, participated in the conception of "Sign, Symbol, Object, Metaphor," the exhibition that was never realized but which in many respects anticipated some of the concerns explored in this exhibition. Anne Ayres, the Museum's former associate curator, spent many patient hours discussing with me both the premise for and possible artists to be included in *OBJECTives*. Most importantly, I greatly benefited from the guidance and support of the Museum's past director, Kevin E. Consey, whose willingness to see this exhibition through many periods of evolution is most appreciated. The sculptor Reinhard Mucha from West Germany, whose monumental sculpture *Gladbeck* we had requested, had an indirect but major impact on the direction of the exhibition. The potential inclusion of *Gladbeck* and my subsequent discussion of this piece with the other artists during the planning stages helped to move my thinking and theirs toward the importance of a contextual placement of the objects/sculpture within specialized environments or installations. Unfortunately, because of commitments made earlier, most importantly to the 1990 Venice Biennale, Mucha was unable to participate.

In the organization of an exhibition, the willingness of artists and lenders to participate is imperative. Of equal significance is the enthusiasm and dedication of the staff that is responsible for researching,

assembling, documenting, registering, installing, publicizing, and administering a project of this size. The Museum is very fortunate to have a team of dedicated individuals who have pursued this exhibition with enormous vigor and professionalism. More than any other staff member, Marilu Knode, Assistant Curator, is responsible for the success of this project. She has been involved with every aspect of organizing this exhibition, working directly with the artists, lenders, essayists and the other staff members. The curatorial staff members who have most directly supported this exhibition include my assistant, Lorraine Dukes, who has handled much of the correspondence, travel coordination, and communication with artists, and Betsy Severance, Registrar, who has dedicated herself to the safe handling and shipment of many difficult works in both Europe and the U.S. Also acknowledged are the contributions of Ellen Breitman, Director of Education, and Karin Schnell, Associate Director of Education, for educational programs; Margie Shackelford, Director of Development, and Kathleen Costello, Associate Director of Development, for development of grants and funding to support the exhibition; Maxine Gaiber, Public Relations Officer, for development of the public relations/publicity program; Jane Piasecki, Associate Director, for the myriad administrative details; and Sandy O'Mara, Graphic Designer, for graphics. Brian Gray, Exhibition Designer, and Richard Tellinghuisen, Director of Operations, receive my heartfelt thanks for the overall design and installation of *OBJECTives*. More than most exhibitions, *OBJECTives* has necessitated a sensitive awareness to and responsibility for the execution of the very specific needs that each artist's installation demanded.

This catalog represents the contributions of many individuals, including the artists themselves, the editor, essayists, researchers, designers and publishers. The *OBJECTives* catalog has been ably compiled and edited by Sue Henger, Museum Editor, with the assistance of Marilu Knode. Additional expertise and support were provided by Peter Kosenko, Gabrielle Daughtry, Dorritt Kirk Fitzgerald, Karene Gould, Lorraine Dukes and Ursula Cyga. David Tanimoto, catalog designer, with the assistance of Rose Ornelas, has created a design that brings an overall clarity and cohesiveness to the individual artist sections within the book. The

Museum has for the second time benefited greatly from the participation of Rizzoli International Publications as copublishers of the hardbound edition. The involvement of William Dworkin of Rizzoli has increased both the quality and dissemination of this catalog.

Without the contributions of art historians, museum curators, and art critics, the scholarly significance of this publication would not have been possible. I am especially grateful to Dan Cameron for contributing an introductory essay and to Kenneth Baker, Lucinda Barnes, Rosetta Brooks, Lynne Cooke, Jean-Pierre Dubost, Peter Schjeldahl, Stephan Schmidt-Wulffen and Elisabeth Sussman for individual essays on the artists. All of the essays were commissioned specifically for this exhibition.

The following institutions, galleries, foundations and individuals provided us with photographic material included in the catalog: Artists Space, New York; Galerie Daniel Buchholz, Cologne; capc, Musée d'art contemporain, Bordeaux; Galerie Gisela Capitain, Cologne; Natasha Sigmund, Paula Cooper Gallery, New York; Deste Foundation for Contemporary Art, Athens; Lynne Sowder, First Bank Minneapolis; Rhona Hoffman Gallery, Chicago; Rafael Jablonka, Jablonka Gallery, Cologne; Kaiser Wilhelm Museum, Krefeld; Kunsthalle Basel, Switzerland; Lia Rumma, Naples; Galería Marga Paz, Madrid; Lawrence Beck, Sonnabend Gallery; Monika Sprüth Galerie, Cologne; Galerie Micheline Szwajcer, Antwerp, Belgium; Galerie 't Venster, Rotterdam; Donald Young Gallery, Chicago.

Many individuals and galleries, although not lenders to the exhibition, helped enormously in its organization of the exhibition. They include: Josh Baer, Josh Baer Gallery, New York; Paula Cooper, Paula Cooper Gallery, New York; Alan Irikura and Mathew Droege of the Haim Steinbach studio, New York; Jörg Johnen, Johnen & Schöttle, Cologne; Marga Paz, Galería Marga Paz, Madrid. Many other individuals and galleries assisted in providing information and materials: Massimo Audiello Gallery, New York; Catherine Little, Brooke Alexander Gallery, New York; John Gibson Gallery, New York; Marian Goodman Gallery, New York; Ghislaine Hussenot, Paris; Galerie Lelong, New York; Luhring Augustine Gallery, New York; Metro Pictures, New York; Peter Pakesch Gallery, Vienna; Katherine David, Centre Georges Pompidou, Paris; and Jamie Wolff, New York.

This exhibition has taken an unusual degree of commitment on the part of its financial supporters and the Board of Trustees. Because of the inability to circulate an exhibition of installation/site-oriented works such as this, the full financial responsibility was borne by the Museum.

The Newport Harbor Art Museum has benefited greatly from the National Endowment for the Arts' initial support for research and development and subsequently from a substantial NEA grant for the implementation of the exhibition.

It is, however, the support of The Irvine Company and its Chairman, Donald Bren, that has ultimately made this exhibition possible. The Irvine Company has made a ten-year commitment to support major exhibitions at the Newport Harbor Art Museum, and this generosity has allowed the Museum to originate such challenging exhibitions as *OBJECTives* and *Chris Burden*, and such historical exhibitions as *The Interpretive Link* and *Action/Precision*.

The opportunity to organize such an exhibition, finally, would not have been possible without the commitment of the Museum's Program Committee, under the leadership of Mrs. Charles Ullman, and the ongoing support for vigorous and original programs by the Board of Trustees.

Paul Schimmel
Chief Curator

Katharina Fritsch
Anthurium, 1989
Installation at *Mondi Possibili*
exhibition, Monika Sprüth
Gallery, Cologne, 1989

OBJECTives

PAUL SCHIMMEL

In 1913 two sculptures were made that anticipated the tension between abstract, naturally evocative sculpture and conceptually charged object making. These masterpieces, Brancusi's head of *The First Step* and Duchamp's *Bicycle Wheel*, are the source, in a general sense, of the difference in the eighties between the group of artists represented in this exhibition, whose work inherits Duchamp's tradition, and sculptors such as Martin Puryear and Robert Therrien, who are closer to the tradition of Brancusi. The debate between these two attitudes about the nature of sculpture has continued throughout the twentieth century. However, seldom in that period has sculpture taken such a central position in the art world as it does today.

OBJECTives: The New Sculpture examines recent tendencies in sculpture through the work of eight artists represented in room-size installations and/or coherent bodies of work. Grenville Davey, Katharina Fritsch, Robert Gober, Jeff Koons, Annette Lemieux, Juan Muñoz, Julian Opie and Haim Steinbach define a new generation of sculpture that is not revisionist in nature but extends the traditions begun by Duchamp with the bicycle wheel placed on a stool.

These artists have by no means signed on with intent to represent the tradition of Duchamp and conceptual objecthood. None of them are purists to the extent that they embrace only one aspect of sculpture. Davey works within a formalist tradition; Fritsch is spiritually inspired; and although Gober may seem the natural inheritor of Duchamp (with his urinals), he is in a sense closer, in touch, to Brancusi than anyone else in this exhibition. Koons, the master of irony, would seem the natural inheritor of pop, but without the conceptual vernacular that emerged during the seventies there would be no structure to his decorative impulses. Annette Lemieux, an artist of words, is clearly linked with the poet and object maker of dada and surrealism; yet without the narrative and conceptual influences of the seventies, her art would lack its peculiar and disorienting effect. Steinbach is the quintessential collector and curator of objects. Without the structure of minimalist sculpture, however, Steinbach would be an anthropologist. The viewpoint these artists have in common, a fascination with the evocative power of mundane or overlooked forms,

marks a turn away from the abstract and universal to a more personal, psychological, economic, and political relationship with the object.

This exhibition suggests a new sculptural realism. It is a realism as skewed as surrealist or pop images of the past, but the primary objective of these artists is to make three-dimensional a concept—to make real a thought. They reject nature, the biomorphic, and primitive art as sources as they eschew the expressive modeling and formal touch of much recent sculpture.

For this exhibition Gober, Muñoz, Fritsch, Opie, and Steinbach have created specialized installations. Surprisingly, without any collaboration, three of the artists have included wall or floor coverings in their rooms. Muñoz, well known for his patterned floors, has designed one specifically for this exhibition based on the geometric pattern on the scaly backs of two bronze dragons that flank the entryway to his room. Gober's reinstallation of the door and door frame—with, for the first time, his playpen and plywood panel—includes the recently created wallpaper based on a pattern originally used on the pillow in one of the dogbed sculptures (1986-87). Steinbach has chosen a moiré patterned fabric for the walls surrounding his monumental boxed sculpture.

The search for a subject in the 1980s has led many of these artists not to elevating subjects or materials but to reconfiguring the commonplace and conventional. The hardware store, not the art supply shop, has provided common, available, and non-class-distinctive resources. Whereas pop art glorified the products of a generation electrified by its own ability to communicate and sell to the masses, this generation doesn't care. Why bother elevating the logos of the corporate world to a level of high art? Explore the hardware store, images of the mass culture.

A curious amalgamation of materials makes up the oeuvre of the artists in *OBJECTives*. Grenville Davey's flattened circular objects—resembling enlarged bottle caps, covers, mirrors, and buttons—comment on the prevalence of this form in our man-made environment. Fritsch has fashioned racks of merchandise, a catalog of objects for sale, and dishes and furniture that one might find in a housewares department. Gober's sinks, doors, drains, plywood panels, and wallpaper are the stuff of serious home remodeling. Lemieux salvages used objects, altering items such as furniture, books, hats, and rugs. Koons, forever industrious, has enshrined and encased stacks of vacuum cleaners—shop-vacs, canisters, and uprights. Muñoz chooses linoleum, wood, and durable paint for his patterned floors and fashions banisters and balconies, objects that serve well in public buildings. Opie's oversized night lights are the stuff of dreams for a hardware man—switches, fans, fuses, toggles, vents, and fixtures. All are functional but do nothing. Steinbach, the consummate consumer, doesn't bother to transform his enigmatic purchases; he builds formica shelves and boxes for them and calls it a day.

These artists, having in most cases grown up in the sixties, were very likely aware of the esthetic battle taking place in their homes: that is, the war between modern, contemporary, clean, well-designed international style and chintz—that ever-present malignancy of the poorly designed object, airport art, plastic slipcovers, and tchotchkes. These college-educated artists, with their good esthetic manner, have not only turned their backs on the cool, clean minimalism of the modern style, they have gone on to embrace its antithesis. The rooms in this exhibition are littered with the esthetic equivalent of plastic-covered sofas. It is not just a question of high versus low art, it is more like bad versus good taste. The pop artists elevated commercial subjects, but these artists are not nearly so heroic in their aspirations; the pop artists had to respond to the abstract expressionist generation, while this generation is responding to conceptual and minimal art.

In the process of making art out of common subjects and objects, the artists in *OBJECTives* transform, metamorphose, alter, and recontextualize the objects into another reality. Given the conventionality of the subjects, for the most part, there is a large dose of fantasy, a dreamlike quality in the resulting sculpture. The common becomes a nightmare. This is not a spiritual art per se, but for a jaded group of art professionals, which this generation can't help but be, the work is infused with considerable nostalgia, whimsy, disorientation, and surreality. Lemieux's typewriters spit out musical texts, her globes become books, and her books create texts from titles. Koons's equalization tanks present the impossible, with basketballs suspended above, at, or beneath the waterline; his cast-bronze lifevest and inflatable boat function about as well as Meret Oppenheim's fur-lined cup. Plastic rabbits just don't become stainless steel, and porcelain was not intended for statues of the gods of our time, such as Michael Jackson. Wrong subject, right material—or right subject, wrong material.

The world is not populated with displaced balconies and handrails, ventriloquist dummies, and dragons, as Muñoz's subjects of vicious fantasies would suggest. Gober, starting with his sinks, has attempted to disorient the viewer. And with each new subject he has advanced his journey into a completely remade, artificial environment of visual non sequiturs

English sculptors Opie and Davey both physically enlarge their subjects. In a world of giants Opie's night lights and Davey's caps and covers would be properly scaled. Finally, like three-dimensional surrealist paintings, Steinbach's constructions juxtapose objects from different contexts, yet without the visual tricks of surrealist montage. In surrealist painting, the viewer can read meaning into objects through their relation to each other and to the fictive environment they occupy. Steinbach's objects, however, defy such a conventional reading.

When Davey was first selected for this exhibition, it was his more representational steel painted sculptures that were considered: *Rail* (1987), with its oblong, racetrack shape; *Grey Seal* (1987), with its dual references to Brancusi's seal and to the seal on a glass bottle of soda. But these quickly led to the recent series of works with their greater physicality. Whereas earlier works alluded more specifically to man-made objects, the new works reveal more about their own making. Davey's tops, caps, and covers are now twisted and ripped apart; they dance between the pop tradition of Oldenburg and the formalist tradition of English sculpture as best exemplified in the work of Anthony Caro. The works, no longer representing real objects, are about the process of building and dismembering.

More than any other artist in this exhibition, Katharina Fritsch is emotionally, psychologically, and spiritually attached to her sculptures. Certainly the other artists are involved with their subjects, but Fritsch's sculptures seem more personal, less about esthetics, politics, and art history than other works in the exhibition. Fritsch, like the nineteenth-century symbolists, creates works that manifest the impossible, the dreamlike, the ideal attained when subject, form, and color unite to materialize an image held in the mind. Like a tonalist painter, she endows each object with an uninflected color that embodies her feeling about the subject: a yellow madonna, a red book, a green elephant—and a gray shark is yet to come. These are not images she dreamed up but ones culled from memory. Together they form a personal narrative. They attempt to make something loaded and charged into something banal—one would never see a green elephant, for example, except as a Fritsch sculpture. Fritsch's ghost in *Ghost and Pool of Blood* is how we collectively imagine a ghost to look, but there is nothing real about it except the viewer's belief in it.

Although Duchamp's urinal and Gober's urinals might seem to have sprung from the same impulse, their intentions differ more than their similarities would suggest. Duchamp's is a readymade, a found or purchased object recontextualized in a manner similar to Koons's vacuum cleaners and Steinbach's lava lamps. Gober's handcrafted urinals, however, are related to the sculptural tradition of Brancusi, with attention to modeling, surface, and texture. Where Duchamp's work is about the object itself, Gober's is about the process of the object's creation. These are not products of a master craftsman. The playpen or the door and doorframe would have no history, no resonance, no meaning if they were honed to perfection. The playpen, with its awkward, chewed-up, slept-in quality, has a soul. Gober's sculptures work on a number of levels, as evidenced in one of the starkest works included in this exhibition, a handbuilt replica of a commercial plywood panel. It *is* what you see—laminated fir. It is also the ultimate minimalist sculpture, casually leaning against a wall, deriving its significance from the context in which it has been placed.

If Jeff Koons did not already exist, the art world would have had to invent him. Perhaps we did. Certainly Koons would have us believe that we did, that he is a mere reflection of our needs and desires, and that, through the looking glass—Jeff—we find an image of fulfillment. As Koons likes to point out, someone in every generation has to be held up as the shining example of what is wrong with current art. It is a dirty job, but Koons, who has the singlemindedness of a missile, has taken on the duty. Koons's conceptual strategy is to reveal his ambition.

The ten cast stainless steel sculptures in this exhibition are frozen, metamorphosed images of subjects that encompass a range of esthetic values from the highest decorative impulse to the lowest commercial banality. Koons starts with *Louis XIV* as the highest form of French Rococo art: the image of the Sun God, the builder of France's great monarchy, the controller of the kingdom and the esthetics of his period. Sliding down the scale between *Louis XIV* and *Rabbit*, the most banal and commercial of the images, Koons offers *The Italian Woman*, bucolic, fanciful, surrounded by flowers and rivers, embracing nature, and in her bountifulness a natural phenomenon herself; *Two Kids*, a scene in the tradition of seventeenth-century Dutch genre painting, little children in an intimate scene of daily life. Sinking lower in the range, *Cape Codder Troll* and *Mermaid Troll* mimic the kind of rough-hewn wooden knick-knacks one might buy on seaside trips and, ideally, leave somewhere on the side of the road before reaching home. Somehow it is appropriate that it is not the "highest" cultural artifact, the Louis XIV statue, that has reached the most sensational dollar value; it is the lowest form, the transformed, inflatable rabbit. *Rabbit* has become, in the four years since its creation, the masterpiece of the infamous show at Sonnabend Gallery that introduced Koons, Steinbach, Peter Halley, Meyer Vaisman, and Ashley Bickerton to a significantly larger audience than they had in the East Village. The casual folds, seams and creases of the plastic bunny from which the statue was created are forever fixed. The sculpture also reflects all that surrounds it. It may not have been Koons's intention, but no doubt it was his desire that all the other art in that exhibition would remain mere reflections in the greatness of this masterful rabbit, the tenth and final work of Koons's stainless steel statues.

Annette Lemieux is becoming known as the master of the tightly selected "group" show. The frequent response on first viewing a Lemieux exhibition is to wonder how many artists have participated. This is understandable, given the fact that the least of her interests is consistency of image or the creation of a signature style. Working with found objects, words, and appropriated images of a nostalgic nature, Lemieux creates poetic narratives out of her symbolic objects. In *Showing One's Colors*, Lemieux has created an emblem, a battle flag that announces to the art world that she, like Barnett Newman, is not afraid of red, yellow and blue. This exhibition brings together works related to the theme of intelligence. The titles of *Two Short Stories* and *Tall Tale* describe both the form and the content of the works. *Sonnet* moves the viewer's eye through the sculpture in a nonlinear fashion. Lemieux's titles often assist the viewer to grasp the ironic edge of her sculptural investigation. *Domino Theory*, an elegant spiral of books, becomes a physical manifestation of the political thesis that tends to whirlpool the U.S. into pointless military conflict. Yet instead of addressing geopolitical strategy, the books are concerned with unity, psychology, philosophy, and anthropology, suggesting the idea that if one aspect of our understanding of human nature were pulled out, our whole structure of knowledge would collapse.

Like Katharina Fritsch, Juan Muñoz materializes the imaginary, inventing dwarf and puppet figures, fanciful dragons, and handrails to nowhere. Muñoz first came to international attention with the handrail sculptures, segments of wooden banisters—ordinary at first, then incorporating increasingly elaborate embellishments. These works anticipated Muñoz's later figurative impulses in that they so strongly beckon human interaction. Prior to the rails, Muñoz had made a series of elevated iron balconies, which led him to a more comprehensive use of the exhibition space. In response to the balconies, he began to paint decorative patterns on the floor, creating optically disorienting environments. Muñoz's floors have a hallucinogenic effect, suspending reality and prompting a more open attitude toward the odd figurative characters that occupy the space. His vicious little people are psychomechanical humans with fierce intentions. The balconies, floors, and puppets mark Muñoz as an object maker, an installation artist, and a figurative sculptor in a neoconceptual world.

Julian Opie's abstract-pop, nearly perceptual light-and-space sculptures, the *Night Lights*, are a little like Robert Ryman paintings in drag. Their elegant surfaces of frosted glass, representing transparent turns of light, seem to emphasize the tradition of Monet's rapturous explorations into the density of light on cathedrals and haystacks. And like Larry Bell's electrocoated glass sculptures, Opie's recent works seem to be investigations of perceptual phenomena. In fact, the *Night Lights* are really about hardware—light bulbs and fans, pushbuttons and toggles, nuts, bolts and washers, plugs, cords and outlets. They make the sublime ridiculous. They take the seriousness out of serious art.

While sixties minimalism was the basis of Haim Steinbach's formative years, seventies conceptualism was his background. Instead of dreaming nostalgically about the purity of things before commercialism usurped the art world, Steinbach knew those years first-hand and seems to relish consumerism of the new age. The most theoretical of the group, Steinbach has taken objects initially from the commercial and industrial world and more recently from both primitive and folk art sources, and placed them within systems and structures that reveal their antecedents: the triangulated shelf form

clearly refers to such sculptures as Donald Judd's "wall progressions." For Steinbach, early-eighties expressionism, with its emotionally charged subjects and style, was no answer to the death of painting; rather, it seemed a mistake, an interruption in sculpture's continuing history. Instead of reacting against eighties neofigurative tendencies, his work simply ignores them. In his most recent works, the two-sided freestanding constructions, Steinbach creates increasingly complex, three-dimensional manifestations of his sculptural syntax. Now the viewer no longer reads left to right; he has to remember and compare opposite sides.

In *OBJECTives* realist sculpture based on the object takes on a double duty, representing both itself and the society from which it sprang. The surrealists seemed more fully transformative in their treatment of objects, while the artists here straddle the fence between the concrete world of commonplace objects and a conceptual arena embracing surrealist dream and fantasy on one hand and political, social, and economic reflection on the other.

These artists do not present a revolution in sculpture so much as a natural evolution from seemingly disparate sources. It would seem impossible to make an object that embraces the dada and surrealist tradition, minimalism, and conceptual art, but that is exactly what this generation has done. They have created an art in which objects function as words, words function as images, and images become a background to a new artistic society where the challenge is to co-opt before being co-opted. They proceed to outflank the collectors, curators, and critics, to create an art that accepts the commercial, postmodern, electronic age in which we live, and to assert at the same time that it is still possible to be a poet, a politician, a sociologist, a religious fanatic, or a dreamer.

View of *Cultural Geometry* exhibition, designed by Haim Steinbach for Deste Foundation for Contemporary Art, Athens

HISTORY IN TRANSLATION: NOTES ON RECENT U.S. AND EUROPEAN SCULPTURE

DAN CAMERON

From the beginning of the 1980s up to the eve of the nineties, the importance of sculpture in the development of new artistic forms and ideas has gradually increased to an exponential degree, far beyond what the actual lapse of years would suggest. Looking back at such landmark exhibitions of the early eighties as *Zeitgeist* or *A New Spirit in Painting*, one is struck not so much by the overall shift in sensibility between then and now as by the curious fact that virtually all the important positions of that moment were being staked out by artists whose commitment to the loaded paintbrush was deemed to be critically unassailable. As if to emphasize the rupture between the freeform artistic meanderings of the seventies and the dawn of an ostensibly new era, the mostly expressionist paintings which began to flood the international art arena some ten years ago made a point of wearing their historical self-consciousness on their sleeves (although in retrospect one might also observe that the odds of being smiled upon by posterity have always been overwhelmingly in favor of painters). At the close of the modern era, painting was a breathless expression of both denial and self-indulgence, of rigid principles and extravagant liberties.

Looking at the international panorama of art production as it exists today, it is hard to recall what all the commotion was about. Serious international painting exhibitions are so rare nowadays as to be literally an endangered species, while massive sculpture surveys—especially of the outdoor, public variety—have become one of the flashier museological trends in Europe over the last few years. More to the point, perhaps, is the degree to which the sculpture of the present day has completely redefined itself in terms of articulating the complex symbiotic relationship between the world of art and the world of everyday reality—not unlike the way in which late-conceptual photography sought to bridge the philosophical gap between mass-produced images and the perilously balanced status of the unique, handmade object. In light of the urgency with which contemporary sculpture seems to make its presence felt, one could safely say that, all other things being equal, if Warhol were a young artist emerging at the end of the eighties, he would almost certainly be making sculpture instead of painting.

It almost goes without saying, then, that the present-day situation is evidence of the more fundamental struggle over representational meaning which exists beneath the surface of all abrupt transformations in public taste. At its best, the work of the newest American and European sculptors is strangely mercurial, continually shifting its weight between the declarative, formal values of traditional modernist sculpture and the more critical urge to challenge art's value system on its own terms. One could explain this uneasy confluence in part by observing that all three-dimensional things, like sculptures, integrate themselves into their environment in a way that pictures cannot. Since it exists in real—as opposed to symbolic—space, and can therefore be more easily mistaken for something which is not art, sculpture which aspires toward objecthood also lends itself quite readily to a process of internal subversion of the art work's signifying power. Yet, because of this same dual role, so-called "critical" sculpture must function superbly as an object before it can ever be deemed ready to undermine the value system on which sculpture depends.

In discussing the critical tendencies that infuse the work of Katharina Fritsch or Annette Lemieux as deeply as that of Jeff Koons or Haim Steinbach, it is important to stand on slightly firmer ideological ground. With their use of source material which is both public and private at the same moment, these artists clearly differentiate themselves from their photo-appropriationist generation—Sherrie Levine or Louise Lawler, for example—whose practice is more directly tied into deconstructing the distribution system of art objects. By contrast, Robert Gober, Lemieux and Fritsch are artists who prefer to get as deeply "inside" their subjects as possible, manifesting all the ambivalence which they themselves might feel about the issues which those subjects represent. Fritsch is fascinated by the Church in much the same way that Koons is fascinated by Michael Jackson: as a center of a universal hypersignification that draws people's attention out of themselves and onto an "other" that is bigger and more perfect than they. And as artists bound to parallel systems of fetishization, both Fritsch and Koons choose not to pretend that they are in any position to confront their subjects on equal ideological terms.

However, the term "critical" can nevertheless be used to describe the majority of these artists' work, in the sense that their main preoccupation as a group is with blurring, or appearing to blur, the distinctions between sculpture and object in order to bring certain questions about esthetic value into clearer

focus. Even when this subterfuge takes place within the context of a set of clearly established stylistic principles—as in the work of Grenville Davey or Annette Lemieux—the artist's intention is still part of an effort to articulate the gap that exists between the stylized "reality" of contemporary art and the less ambiguous reality of objects, money, work, people and machines. Davey simulates the "friendly" shapes of a hyper-industrialized world in such a way as to bring an ironic anthropomorphism to bear on the exhibition space itself, thereby making the viewer overly conscious of the false neutrality which art often wraps about itself. Lemieux's use of homespun or otherwise humanized objects allows her to catch the viewer off guard for the complex and often sociologically interlaced visual puns that are concealed just below the surface.

To understand how contemporary sculpture arrived at its present state of ambivalent representation, we should first quickly scan the last few decades of its development. Following World War II, French artists of the *nouveau réalisme* movement developed a vocabulary consisting largely of accumulations of objects, street debris and other signs of so-called proletarian culture to produce striking "slice-of-life" assemblages. From Arman's obsessive "still-lifes" and Daniel Spoerri's frozen tableaux, the outer boundaries of esthetics were reached with the absolutist vision of Yves Klein, whose anti-art gestures attempted to freeze manifesto and object into a single cathartic moment. While the idea of everyday objects manipulated by the artist had begun with Duchamp and the Cologne dadaists nearly forty years earlier, the expression of this esthetic in early fifties Europe signaled a strange restlessness concerning the modernist enterprise that stretched across generations, from Meret Oppenheim's oblique object-poems to Marcel Broodthaers' pointed investigation into the nature of esthetic reality. Parallel to this development was the rupture in postwar Italian art which produced both the "spatial concept" reliefs of Lucio Fontana and the curiously neutral "achromes" of Piero Manzoni, whose late-sixties project of canning his own feces became the ultimate conceptual art gesture. Although both Fontana and Manzoni began as painters, the radicality of their gestures spilled over into the concerns of artists working in other media and from completely different cultures.

In America, Robert Rauschenberg's unbridled "combine" structures appeared to link the Paris generation of the fifties with the spirit of frontier abstraction found in Pollock, at the same time paying attention to the mounting hegemony of American media culture in the Western world during the postwar period. However, neither Rauschenberg's art nor the West Coast assemblage school of the same period prepared the audience of the early sixties for the first total expression of the American sensibility through the medium of art: pop. Although they are as indebted to Duchamp and surrealism as they are to the *nouveaux réalistes* and the British pop artists of the late fifties, pop artists in the U.S. broke the barrier of esthetic innovation by aggressively recontextualizing the cultural meaning of art to focus on the youth-oriented, media-based phenomenon of suburban American culture. Interestingly, Andy Warhol, who remains the most important single influence on American artists working today, barely produced any sculpture at all during his career, unless of course you include his very presence. In fact, despite occasional three-dimensional efforts by Roy Lichtenstein or Tom Wesselman, the entire pop generation produced only one major sculptor, Claes Oldenburg, and a few others who were either not really major (George Segal) or not really pop (Edward Kienholz). Yet Warhol's influence is decisive in his having captured a spirit of frustration with the gaps between museum and popular culture and in his having channeled this into a type of liberated object-making, one which insisted on seeing mystery in the superficial and profundity in the banal. By seeming to watch and accept everything, Warhol served not only as antecedent to sculptors like Jeff Koons, Robert Gober, and Haim Steinbach, who work with found materials and forms, but also as model for the numerous artist-as-sociologist and artist-as-curator projects which proliferate today.

Following closely on the heels of pop, sculpture enjoyed a decade-long predominance in the vanguard of American art, threatened only by the short-lived wave of so-called "lyrical abstraction" in the early seventies. As a formal development that rivals pop in the breadth and totality of its rupture with earlier movements, minimalism did away with most of sculpture's traditional precepts: detail, the gradual building up of form, the armature and pedestal, even the most basic notions of articulated space. Instead, minimalist sculpture took the scale and conditions of late-industrialized society as its model, creating solid monoliths of blankness that defied the viewer to establish a psychological scale that bore any relation to the contemporary setting of art (i.e., a home or museum). Although the influence of Carl Andre, Dan Flavin, Donald Judd, Robert Morris, and Richard Serra can be seen in any number of artists working today (including many of the sculptors included in the present exhibition), their work viewed in retrospect seems to mark a turning point in the development of American art to the extent that sculptors were already showing signs of retreating in the direction of a more humanist presence in their work. In fact, minimalist art is in many ways the last tangible gasp of the modernist spirit within the avant-garde, marking a point where formal and theoretical innovation finally painted itself into a corner. Despite the fact that the conceptual art generation of Joseph Kosuth, Robert Barry, Lawrence Weiner, and Douglas Heubler is generally included next in thumbnail surveys of sculpture, under present circumstances it is probably no longer worthwhile to continue classifying their work as "sculpture," since what these artists have accomplished is nothing less than the codification of a completely new tradition—that of the photo/text installation—which today has at least as many practitioners as painting.

Although the most characteristic art movement of the sixties was probably Fluxus, such a mingling of the international avant-garde should be seen less as a time when new forms and ideas emerged than as an expression of a more relaxed relationship between such media as art, music, literature and theater, as well as the first glimmerings of the international sensibility which seems to have lain dormant for a quarter-century before irrevocably taking hold of the art world's imagination. The same cannot be said, however, of *arte povera*, which remains the most concentrated phenomenon of sculptural innovation in Europe in the past half-century. *Arte povera*, whose birth was linked to the manifestations of social unrest of 1967 and 1968, was a more ideologically based expression of similar cultural tendencies, in the sense that in spirit it became a complete rejection of the industrialized techniques and inhuman scale established by the American minimalists. However, far from producing a mere exercise in recycled forms, the *arte povera* artists sought to produce an art that neither rejected the modest conditions of street and political culture in favor of an exaggerated presence known as "art," nor degraded the weighty presence of history and culture in favor of headily pursuing an elitist avant-gardism. Another factor that distanced them from the art of the U.S. during the same period was their comparative lack of influence outside Italy: although Giovanni Anselmo, Luciano Fabro, Jannis Kounellis, Mario Merz, Giulio Paolini and Michelangelo Pistoletto received attention for recycling "poor" materials into confrontational, situational events, their value as artists has only been recognized internationally in the eighties.

Serving as a member of many of the crossover groups of his time, yet completely outside the influence of any of his contemporaries, Joseph Beuys was such a great influence on the art of mid-century that it is impossible to consider the phenomenon of sculpture in the last ten years without thinking of his work. Essentially the result of a utopian artist's vision, one who believed that art is the highest and most urgent form of communication, Beuys's work far transcends the traditional categories of sculpture, yet his influence can be seen fully today in the recurring problems of representation versus expression as they appear in the work of innumerable artists working with objects and sites, both within and outside Germany. For Beuys, the object metamorphosed was a type of transfiguration of internal experience which could not be limited by the formal restrictions of late-modernist art. His ideas opened the way toward a new understanding of the artist as a socially responsible agent of higher discourse, and the current profusion of significant sculptors in Germany—Imi Knoebel, Reinhard Mucha, Rebecca Horn, Wolfgang Laib, Katharina Fritsch, Günter Förg, Rosemarie Trockel, Martin Kippenberger, Hubert Kiecol and Georg Herold, among others—would be unthinkable without Beuys's enduring presence through his emphasis on a direct, sometimes confrontational, discourse.

The monolithic impact of minimalism was followed in the U.S. by the subtler postminimalist generation of the early seventies, and a shift of interest toward more organic or system-based thinking on the part of artists such as Vito Acconci, Mel Bochner, Eva Hesse, Dennis Oppenheim, Robert Irwin, Richard Tuttle, Sol Lewitt, Bruce Nauman, Walter de Maria, and Robert Smithson. As befits its epithet—many of these artists can just as easily be classified as minimalist or conceptual—postminimalism was more of a loosely held cluster of ideals and attitudes than a group of artists held together by shared beliefs. As noncentered as it may have seemed, certain esthetic emphases from the period—such as Smithson's belief that the meaning of sculpture rests entirely on a complex interaction within a specific situation—seem as meaningful today as nearly twenty years ago. Still more importantly, postminimalism may have begun the swing of the stylistic pendulum back toward the suspended state of historical anxiety in which art finds itself even to-day, at a point in time when end-of-millenium pressure seems to mock art's vain attempts to reinvent itself, if only for another season or two.

Reviewing what has happened in the last few years—when a new generation of American and European artists has come to be dominated by sculptors—one is tempted to explain it away by stating that the winds of historical self-consciousness that transformed painting at the end of the seventies needed more time to take effect on sculpture, which is less involved with illusion and thus does not feel quite the same burden of tradition. In fact, it is probably just as true to suggest that so-called postmodern painting was really nothing more than a first attempt to come to terms with the end of the Age of Innovation. Although the first decisive break with this philosophy of art-making can be seen in the early appropriationist photographs of Richard Prince, Sarah Charlesworth, and Sherrie Levine, the earliest indication that the stylistic gap between sculpture and other forms of art exist as a conceptual vacuum (which transcends the traditional limits of media altogether) came in the work of a generation of British sculptors who were catapulted from obscurity to international fame in the short span of years between 1981 and 1985.

In fact, the most available link between recent art history and current sculpture is the work of Tony Cragg, Barry Flanagan, Richard Long, Bill Woodrow, Richard Deacon, Michael Craig-Martin, The Boyle Family, David Nash, Anish Kapoor, Shirazeh Houshiary, Ian Hamilton Finlay, Alison Wilding, Anthony Gormley, Julian Opie, and Richard Wentworth. Whereas certain of these artists—Finlay, Long and Flanagan foremost—had been active since the sixties, almost none of this work was known outside the U.K. before the double wave of British sculpture caught the world by surprise. While variation of ideas and techniques becomes essential within such a large group, an important quality in virtually all of this work is the consideration given to the innate qualities of objects and materials prior to their reworking as sculpture. Whether it is the consideration of abstracted forms

(Kapoor, Wilding), allegorical symbols (Long, Finlay), recycled detritus (Cragg, The Boyles), or the propensity of Caro-generation sculptors to linger over their seams (found today in Deacon or Gormley), a recurring problem in recent British sculpture is the enigma of the object which can never be depleted of its innate interest as a tool and token of the human spirit. Taken collectively, the nature of this group's investigation was to determine whether or not a mixed stylistic repertoire of forms and techniques would speak as clearly through sculpture as the spirit of formal innovation had done only a decade earlier.

As seen in this generation's work, the critical problem which European and American sculptors inherited from the period 1950-1975 was the failing regimen of theoretical ideas which had propelled art through the sometimes breathless changes that mark the postwar period. By 1980 painting had already taken refuge from the failures of modernism by cloaking itself in its sometimes glorious, sometimes tattered, past; but sculpture—which had in fact been the vehicle for art's most radical changes after the early sixties—was left with the sole option of picking through the debris of the preceding quarter-century and piecing together something that allowed for innovation while keeping certain threads of continuity intact. We see one solution in the work of Julian Opie, who at an early age has already developed a chameleonlike approach to the problem of personal style. In effect, each phase of his work serves as a platform for acting through various problems of late twentieth-century art, except that these have been transformed into conceptual gestures that characterize the artwork as a type of container and sculpture as a technique for articulating its requirements. The related ideas of emptying out and filling up seem to present themselves more forcefully in Opie's works of the last two years, which have adopted the position of simulating art objects in the manner of the new American artists.

In contrast, the work of Grenville Davey or Juan Muñoz—which has only been known to general audiences for a couple of years—plumbs more deeply into modernist issues of psychological metaphor, while also sensitizing itself to problems of subtlety and complexity in the way in which art situates itself according to the world of things. Davey, who has developed a hybrid system of forms that balances precariously between the minimalist "site'" and the pop-related hypermagnification of such everyday objects as electrical switches, is the first of a new generation of British sculptors who prefer to strike a relaxed accord between modernist history and the troubled waters of representation. Muñoz, a Spaniard whose work is nevertheless closely linked to the English, Italian and Flemish schools, also draws on the emotional tension that played such an important role in the early work of such American sculptors as Acconci, Nauman and Oppenheim. His installations, which freely mix figurative and architectural elements, seem almost Baroque in their attention to nuance, detail and relative scale and Hitchcockian in their deceptive use of narrative.

The American sculptors whose work seems to have sounded the death knell for early eighties painting—Robert Gober, Jeff Koons, and Haim Steinbach—were at first closely linked together because of their related interest in using objects to create a confrontational situation between the spectator and his/her expectations of esthetic distance. The shock created by these artists' work when it first appeared was closely related to the remystification of the artist's psyche during the preceding years, at which time the dissembling, shamanistic

personalities of painters like Julian Schnabel or Enzo Cucci became at least as important a factor in the reception of their work as the work itself. In his 1985 series incorporating basketballs suspended in aquariums, Koons responded directly to what he perceived as the public's mania for having its beliefs defied. Substituting a floating orb for the more common "miracle" of encrusted paint, Koons provoked the viewer to see the simplicity behind the creative act, while at the same time providing his or her need for an objective spectacle. Steinbach's art, with clear roots in the installation sculpture of the seventies, began as an investigation into rooms and displays, with an anthropologist's detached interest in experiencing that which is typical for a given situation. In time, his shelves with displayed objects came into being as a form of portable site where some form of authentic cultural exchange takes place. The primary difference in the two artists' work lies in the relation between Koons's interest in illusion—in the forces which persuade a viewer to invest faith in an object of art—and Steinbach's involvement in setting up situations in which the viewer is persuaded that all of the dynamics are clearly visible—an experience, in other words, of authenticity once removed.

Whereas the work of both Koons and Steinbach—and, by association, Davey and Opie as well—prides itself in an almost antiseptic clarity, the sculpture of Robert Gober and Annette Lemieux appears first fraught with the complex of anxieties and misgivings that come with being a modern human being. Gober's early sinks and latrines, modeled into existence from plaster and wire armatures, clearly emphasized the use of the artist's hand, thus also suggesting the crucial element of a mortal presence in the work. In a sense, they were substitute characters, studies for lives which had never existed yet were conveyed somehow by these modest forms and appliances. In contrast, Lemieux's first works seemed frivolous, reminiscent of the Duchampian games in Sherrie Levine's art. Soon, however, her sculptures began addressing themselves more specifically to knottier problems of textual illusion, self-deception, and the type of double meanings that always collapse upon themselves or backfire on the subject. Not unlike the books which she often incorporates into her installations, Lemieux's work typically displays both the more official reading and the more subversive subtext. In recent years, both Gober and Lemieux have come to typify a strain in American art that—not unlike the work of Muñoz—sees the complex interweave of private, social, and esthetic meanings within the art work as being a positive rather than a negative factor. In particular, a subdued but always present state of psychological violence—in Gober's use of death-and-sex images or Lemieux's parables of war and gender—gives an accurate account of the demoralized state of Western civilization after coping with nearly ten years of Ronald Reagan and AIDS.

Compared with these artists, Katharina Fritsch is something of an outsider in that she delves with complete lack of irony into the relationship between religious iconography and the reductivist tendencies of twentieth-century abstraction. Although none of her works is abstract, they fall somewhere between the fabricated perfection of Koons's art and the easy trace of the hand found in Gober. Simply put, Fritsch does not frame the everyday icon but presents it unblemished in the form of a relic of modernism, asking the viewer to merge two forms of perception— critical and metaphysical—into one. Like Koons, Fritsch has incurred the wrath of her colleagues by proposing that the quality of belief—formulated and approved by the community that is affected—is more essential to the act of esthetic (or mystical) transference than the objective meaning of the object in question, and that the state of assumed authority is a necessary condition for actualizing this characteristic. By making it patently clear what they are doing, both Koons and Fritsch defy their viewers to believe in art while they simultaneously defy us to stop believing in it as well. In the final pass, it is hoped, this style of attenuated ambivalence leads to a state of tolerance, even transcendence, of historically grounded ideas of difference between esthetic, political, and religious contemplation.

Whereas it would seem to be self-contradictory to propose that the art world can, in general, be in the midst of a crisis of meaning at the same time that it is also responsible for such a potent generation of sculptors, both premises are not only true in the present case but also necessarily true. Manifesting their ideas at the tail-end of a century during which art has completely redefined itself some half-dozen times, the artists who make up the present exhibition are the inheritors of an enormous legacy of innovation and change which nonetheless burned itself out through problems that were not exclusively theoretical in nature but ideological as well, dealing with the very essence of change and progress. Paralleling the scientists worldwide who believe that we must undertake the task of redefining the very nature of investigation now that we have uncovered some of the most basic uncertainties as to how our universe is constituted, artists today no longer view the future as a beckoning utopia but rather as a burden which we will be unable to face unless we learn from the mistakes of our recent past. As this century's history is sifted for clues as to what parts of the rubble of modernism are still useful, the artists leading the search appear to display a certain moral ambivalence, perhaps because they are aware that it is not at all certain we will be in a position to reinvest these forms with the idealism that attended their discovery. To paraphrase Marshall McLuhan, both the medium and the message of sculpture (and, by implication, all cultural expression) have become somewhat battered by this century's race to stay one step ahead of itself. This time around, however, our capability for recognizing meaning does not depend on end-game strategies but rather on the unspoken conviction—perhaps just as elusive—that once we have discovered just what it is we are looking for, then half the quest—and not necessarily the most fruitful half—will already be behind us.

PLATES
AND
ENTRIES

GRENVILLE DAVEY

Grenville Davey's sculptures present themselves confidently as large tangible self-contained objects. Whether single or in pairs, they generally confine themselves to a carefully delimited vocabulary. The majority are circular in form and present a dominant face: on the floor they are topside up; on the wall they adhere flat to the plane. Their active engagement with the site of the gallery is at once marked and equivocal. They resemble architectural elements of the urban streetscape, such as lightfittings, manhole covers, or mirrors for facilitating a safe traffic flow, yet they maintain a crucial aura of displacement, given that the art gallery is not the normal venue for such entities.

At one level, these allusions serve to indicate Davey's awareness of the ways in which the context—both physical and linguistic—frames the work of art. The key modernist conception of the gallery or museum as a neutral site was exploded in the sixties when conceptual artists examined the discourses that condition the display of the work of art. Equally undermined was the late modernist notion of the canonical artwork as an autonomous self-referential hermetic object shorn of all signification beyond the literal material facts of its being and the contingencies of its viewing. During the eighties, deference to these acts of deconstruction, and to the lifting of the suppression of both the social and ideological functions of the artwork, has become not only a prerequisite but virtually a routine response on the part of object makers and installation artists alike. If too often this recognition amounts to little more than a paying of one's dues, Davey's sculptures, like Julian Opie's "ventilators" and glass "cabinets" contemporaneously, are ultimately less concerned with the contextualizing of the artwork by the gallery than with the contemporary urban environment and its determining values.[1]

Close examination of Davey's works reveals that they are not readymades; that is, they are not "found" objects. They may be partially composed from industrial elements, but more often, as with *Cover*, the forms have been made to the artist's specifications by industrial fabricators. In *Grey Seal*, however, he has combined a purchased element with a component made to his requirements. And in *Rail*, he has constructed the whole himself. In most of his recent works, Davey again combines procedures: once the annulus has been made to order, he completes the work in the studio through a process of trial and error. If there is no mystique attached to the handmade in his art; conversely, fabrication serves as a means, not primarily as a signifying factor.

His titles range from an initial, laconic acknowledgment of the inherent referentiality of the object (e.g., *Rail*, *Untitled Pair*, *Seal*, and *Cover* of 1987-88) to a growing engagement with its metaphorical potential (e.g., *By Air*, *Labil*, and *Over* of 1989). Compared to the terse, clipped names of 1987-88 the titles are more openended and less specific, no longer perfunctorily admitting association but welcoming it positively.

Davey was a student in London in the early eighties, when Richard Deacon, Tony Cragg and a number of their British peers began making "object-based sculpture." A key issue for these artists was to avoid having their work read as formalist, and hence retrograde, sculpture. It was a particularly acute problem for those who, like Deacon, were employing an apparently abstract morphology with straightforward methods of making, utilizing ordinary, often synthetic, materials. Their particular contribution has been seminal to the reestablishment of

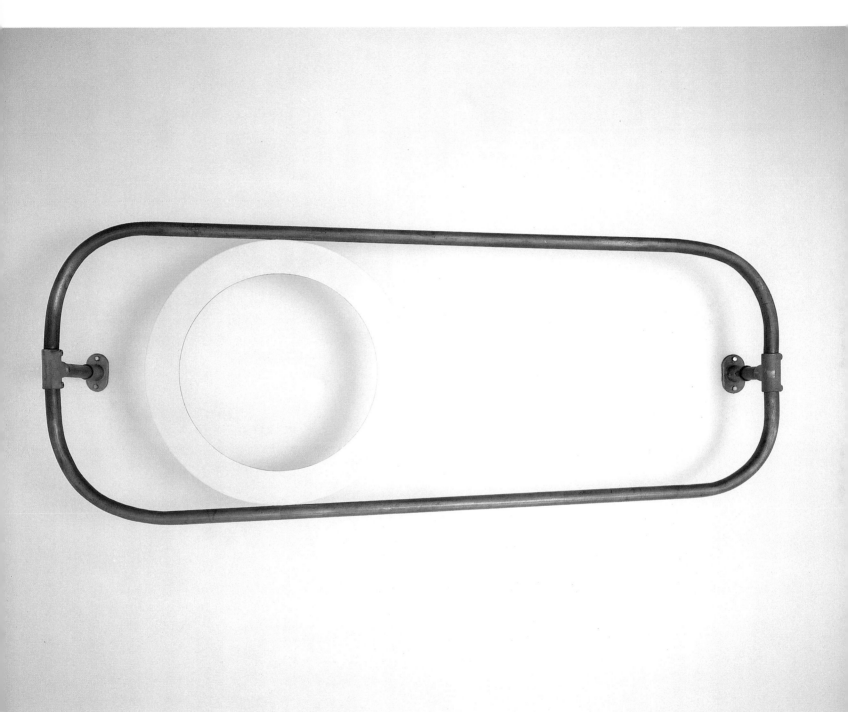

Rail, 1987
stainless steel, steel tube,
rubber cord
39 3/4 x 100 x 2 1/4 in.
(101.5 x 256 x 5.5 cm)
Saatchi Collection, London

making a viable object-based sculpture that addresses concerns fundamental to objects in general and, not least, that dialectic between the art object and other everyday objects.[2]

Maturing under the aegis of Deacon and others gave Davey the conviction that there was still a tenable role for sculpture conceived as a self-contained three-dimensional object. Second, it broke down any remaining barriers between what had hitherto been called abstraction and figuration: all sculptural form is now perceived to be referential and metaphorical. And, finally, it encouraged a direct, straightforward working relationship with commonplace materials. For Davey, as for his immediate predecessors, sculpture was presumed to be a distinct class of entity, one whose members were different from but related to other types of physical objects, especially those that are manufactured. Even more than Deacon's, Davey's works refer to commonplace objects without being actual representations of them.[3] Moreover, in his sculpture, the *act* of making is less important than in Deacon's, though *how* they are made and *from what* they are made remain crucial.

Despite the self-evident factuality of Davey's works, the nature of their existence is brought into question. Because of the way the artist installs them, they have the contingent, temporary air of demonstration pieces, on display but destined for other contexts. Further, because of the way he fabricates them, they sometimes take on the character of models or prototypes, made from materials that merely simulate the effect desired in the final form. If produced in bulk as standardized entities, they would presumably be in metal not hardboard, and the procedures would be more fully automated, involving less handworking than has occurred in the manufacture of these particular "samples," uniform, regular, and anonymous though their finish always is.

Installation at Magasin, Grenoble, 1988. Left: *(Vinyl) Pair*, 1988; Back wall: *Untitled Pair*, 1987; Floor: *Cover II*, 1987.

Such conclusions largely stem from the conviction that the works allude to the modern urban industrial environment. Admittedly, Davey's distinctive morphology conveys quite a diverse range of references, suggesting objects as disparate as lids, switches, gas cylinder tops, architectural members, and mirrors that guide traffic flow at junctions. The fact that they tend to be generic enhances their potential for uniform repeatability and reinforces their identity as typologies. This similarity can ultimately be seen to depend upon the way that standardized procedures and streamlined production have become a hallmark of late twentieth-century industrialized society.

Yet Davey's objects bear little relation to the consumer artifact that has fascinated many object makers in recent years. Nor do they relate to that somewhat different cult, which has become even more of a focus of eighties mentality—the "designer" object. Marked by their fetishization of style, in which the label replaces form as the vehicle for recognition, such commodities are sought and cherished for their ability to betoken a certain taste, lifestyle, and set of values. Davey's objects, by contrast, are not only generic rather than individual but suggest more "primitive" modes of production, ones that create heavy-duty, robust, durable entities—a realm that encompasses the machine shop, engineering works, and high-utility public spaces. Objects found in these spheres are usually not infused with a high level of design intended to give an imprint of artistry. Instead, they are generally forthrightly utilitarian in appearance. Most of his

Untitled Pair, 1987
spun steel, cellulose paint
34 3/4 x 1 3/4 in. each
(89 x 4 cm)
Saatchi Collection, London

works in addition evoke a functionality that requires interaction. Unlike appliances, bottles, tools, and instruments, which are all self-contained entities, lids, covers, lights, switches, caps, brackets, and so forth are normally affixed to larger entities.

Evading precise definition, these sculptures invite being read in the context of architecture—though not of architecture for its own sake but in relation to certain debates that currently imbue it with intense controversy and unprecedented publicity.[4]

Installation at Lisson Gallery, London, 1989. Left: *Right 3rd/6th*, 1989; Right: *By Air*, 1989; Floor: *Runner*, 1989

The modernist and postmodernist arguments that have dominated the architectural community elsewhere over the past two decades have taken on a somewhat different complexion in Britain to the degree that they devolve around considerations of the past glory of Britain ("the heritage industry"), of its former imperial domains, and of its pioneering industrial might: sentiments, nostalgia and even nationalism are implicated in this controversy. A vociferous champion of the pastiching revivalists is the Prince of Wales (who gives the conservative establishment position much specious but nevertheless popular credibility).[5] Possibly his most effective opponents are two internationally celebrated English architects, Richard Rogers and Norman Foster, each of whom can be described as a devotee of an idiosyncratic late modernism. This debate has both widespread and crucial implications because it touches not only architecture, and with it the built environment, but the governing values which the society as a whole promotes. While the encroachments of technological innovation on contemporary society are also currently much discussed, it is not the electronics revolution which most fundamentally alters the face of the built environment but the products of industrial construction: compare, for example, the impact of digital billboards on Piccadilly Circus with that of Rogers's Lloyds building on the streetscapes of the City of London. For the advocates of a modernist related esthetic, a sharper, clearer appreciation of the nature of what is an inescapable and inherently contemporary activity in all its guises, as found in the most ordinary and minute manufactured object as well as in the complex and monumental architectural construction, is desperately called for, together with a recognition of the interconnectedness of all levels and aspects of the built environment.

Grey Seal, 1987
painted steel, steel tube, rubber
cord
13 x 48 3/4 in.
(33 x 124.5 cm)
Saatchi Collection, London

In addressing the technological propensities of modernism, Davey's works situate themselves within this genealogy. Not only do their form and fabrication allude to contemporary means but the materials—spun steel, vacuum-formed plastic, padded vinyl, cellulose paint—are all assertively contemporary. In certain cases, such as *Trommel*, the scale tends to fluctuate dramatically, allowing the work to be apprehended at one moment as something small seen up close, almost as a detail, and at another as something vast. This shift brings with it a recognition of the multiplicity of contexts in which forms like these can be found, the predominance and the ubiquity of standardized elements, and industrial methods of production in the modern material world.

Installation at Lisson Gallery, London, 1989. Left: *Fat Edge*, 1989; Right: *Pair*, 1989; Floor: *Runner*, 1989

When Duchamp selected a bottle rack in 1914, he was concerned principally with emphasizing the role that intellect plays in the creation of the artwork and with the priority it should have over skill, craft, and talent. Subsequently, the plastic qualities of his artifact have provided a set of characteristics which have served as touchstones for the practice of many sculptors while contributing to the esthetic esteem felt almost universally for certain industrial products. If the so-called Machine Age of the twenties consolidated this burgeoning appreciation, its utopianism eventually brought it into disregard. Although Davey's work directs attention to the problematics of the modernist conception of the art object and to the broader issues it raises, more

significant are the questions he addresses concerning the relationship of the art object to the man-made environment. By eschewing direct allusions to commodities in favor of the larger realm of industrial design and production, his works enter into current debates about the environment at large.

A recognition of the urgency, if not the pertinency, of such issues may be attributed to the particularities of the milieu in which Davey matured as an artist. Nonetheless, they are also a fundamental tenet of the larger modernist heritage, especially as it was breached, albeit often only by implication, in the art of the American minimalists of the sixties. That minimalism was never fully confronted in Britain during that decade, whereas pop was widely heralded, has meant, among other things, that issues relating to mass culture and consumerism have long received critical attention there while those that pertain to design and technology have been almost ignored until recently.[6] This has had widespread implications. For example, in recent years few sculptors in Britain have had their work industrially fabricated; most opt for secondhand materials or off-cuts, which they manipulate by hand, rather than for pristine material purchased new, a preference governed not solely by financial considerations. Although (like Opie) Davey generally constructs his works himself, the impeccable finish of his sculptures approximates closely the results of manufactured processes. In engaging with sculpture that addresses its relationship with other contemporary objects, his art embodies a knowing but robustly optimistic vision both of the potential role for contemporary sculpture and of the legacy of the modernist esthetic.

Lynne Cooke

Red Giant, 1988
painted steel
45 3/4 x 3 in.
(117 x 75 cm)
Saatchi Collection, London

NOTES

1. For a fuller discussion of the relationship of Opie's work to urban environments, see Michael Newman, "Undecidable Objects," in *Julian Opie* (London: Lisson Gallery, 1988), n.p.

2. For a discussion of this dialectic, see Rainer Crone and David Moos, "Introduction," in *Objet/Objectif* (Paris: Galerie Daniel Templon, 1989), n.p.

3. For a more comprehensive discussion of the ways in which Deacon's series *Art for Other People* draws on object codes, see Lynne Cooke, "Richard Deacon: Object Lessons," in *Richard Deacon* (London: Whitechapel Gallery, 1988), pp. 7-22.

4. For a summary of these debates, see Jonathan Glancey, "Prince Versus Progress," *The Independent Magazine*, 2 September 1989, pp. 48-50. One measure of the importance of the debate is the enormous attention paid the Centre Pompidou in Paris. Deyan Sudjic writes that "Piano and Rogers' Beaubourg Centre appears on record covers, as the backdrop to television commercials advertising motorcars, even as a film set, and its most conspicuous features have provided the inspiration for everything from fast-food restaurants to factories. To see the building narrowly as architecture, and to discuss its significance only in the traditional academic sense, becomes impossible." *New Directions in British Architecture: Norman Foster, Richard Rogers, James Stirling* (London: Thames & Hudson, 1986). For a discussion of the wider social implications of contemporary architecture, see Michael Rustin, "Postmodernism and Anti-modernism in Contemporary British Architecture," *Assemblage*, February 1989, pp. 89-103.

5. See HRH The Prince of Wales, *A Vision of Britain: A Personal View of Architecture* (London: Doubleday, 1989). See also the rejoinder by Maxwell Hutchinson, President of the Royal Institute of British Architects, *The Prince of Wales: Right or Wrong?* (London: Faber and Faber, 1989).
Marked by an eighteenth-century pastiche facade and modern materials masquerading as traditional ones, Quinlan Terry's Richmond Riverside Development, which is much admired by the Prince of Wales, was described by the American modernist Richard Meier as a building that "ransacks the past, robs the present and obliterates the future" (quoted in Glancey, p. 50).

6. See Brian Wallis, "Tomorrow and Tomorrow and Tomorrow: The Independent Group and Popular Culture," in *This is Tomorrow Today: The Independent Group and British Pop Art* (New York: The Clocktower, 1987), pp. 9-18.

Button, 1988
painted steel
14 x 58 1/2 in.
(36 x 150 cm)
Private collection, London

Labil, 1988
painted steel, rubber
46 x 10 1/4 in.
(117.5 x 26 cm)
Collection Bette Zeigler, New
York

Right 3rd/6th, 1989
painted steel, hardboard
59 1/2 x 24 1/4 in.
(152.5 x 62 cm)
Collection Dakis Joannou,
Athens

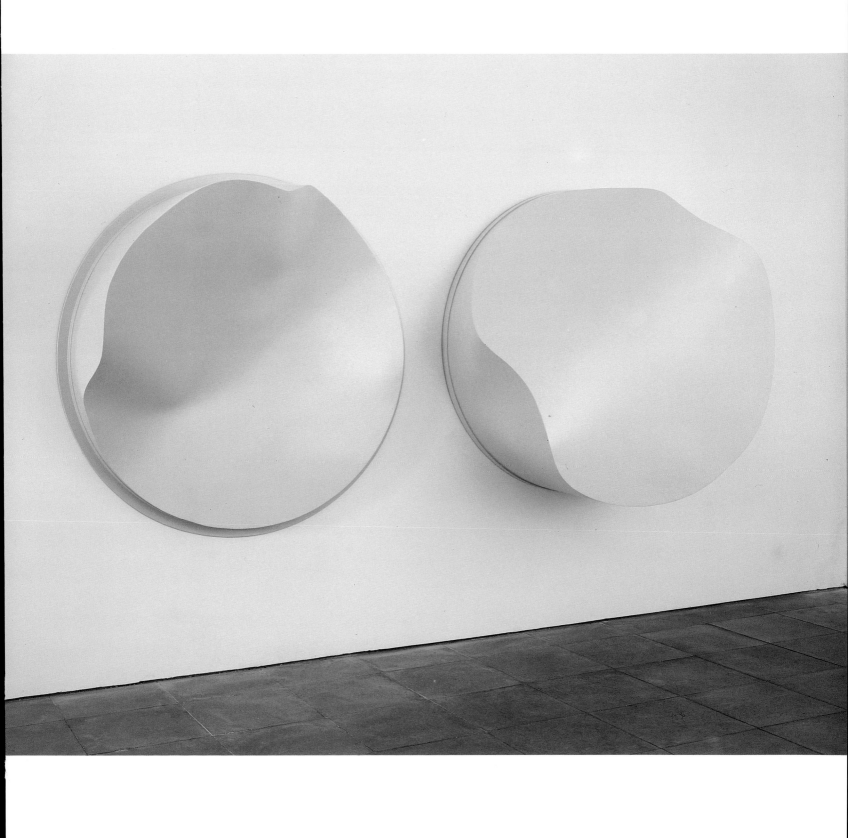

Runner, 1989
rusted mild steel
10 1/2 x 75 3/4 in.
(26.5 x 194 cm)
Collection Jack and
Nell Wendler

By Air, 1989
hardboard, steel
75 x 14 in. each
(192 x 35.5 cm)
Collection Janet Green,
London

Over, 1989
painted steel
39 1/2 x 5 1/4 in. each
(101 x 13 cm)
Collection Janet Green, London

Trommel, 1989
painted steel
10 3/4 x 51 1/2 x in. each
(27 x 131.5 cm)
Lisson Gallery, London

(First), 1989
painted steel
27 3/4 x 8 in.
(70.6 x 20 cm)
Collection Vijak Mahdavi and
Bernardo Nadal-Ginard, Boston

Err (complete), 1989
painted steel
41 1/2 x 9 1/2 in.
(106 x 24 cm)
Lisson Gallery, London

KATHARINA FRITSCH

Whether Mephistopheles or the Virgin Mary, apparitions are information from another world. They merely borrow earthly bodies and are for that reason fascinating. In the familiar daily routine, an unprecedented message lies hidden.

In the summer of 1987, the Virgin Mary appeared in the middle of the Salzstrasse in Münster. Like each of her appearances, this one also had its reason: she was a sculpture by Katharina Fritsch, *Madonna of Lourdes*. The work of art was only a facsimile of a religious appearance which still retains its value in the belief of many citizens of this arch-conservative Catholic city in Westfalia. The madonna figure, life-size, was destroyed the very night it was erected; the same occurred to the replica with which it was replaced. The viewers understood this work as a commentary on their parochial Catholicism. Precisely because Fritsch took the tale of the Mother of God's appearance so literally that she let it become reality, she touched upon a taboo.

Madonna of Lourdes, 1986. Installation at Eaton Centre, Toronto, Canada, polyester resin with plaster base, Collection Ydessa Hendeles, Courtesy Ydessa Hendeles Art Foundation

Rather than select a full-scale church madonna as her model, she chose a pocket-size madonna for sale by the hundreds as a decoration or travel souvenir in the French pilgrim sanctuary of Lourdes. This handy figurine had already appeared in 1984 in Fritsch's *Warengestell mit Madonna (Merchandise Rack with Madonna)*: here, she was presented together with a black-and-white varnished toy car and four white model sheep in front of a crêche, a necklace of red glass beads (which were, however, not threaded), and three artificial anthuriums in glass bottles. In 1981 Fritsch had published a *Werbeblatt (Advertising Prospectus)* in which several of these objects were offered for sale: Order No. 1, the black-and-white car: DM 100,00; Order No. 3, anthuriums: DM 100,00; Order No. 7, wallpaper design: DM 100,00 per square meter. Order No. 9 was the advertising prospectus itself: DM 1,00. This advertising prospectus acted like a kind of masterpiece catalog: many of the works that were offered in it had already appeared in the artist's brief repertoire.

In 1988 the Carnegie Museum of Art in Pittsburgh exhibited a supernatural apparition of another sort. A two-meter-high ghost right out of the pages of a book—a white sheet under which human contours could still be discerned—was installed not far from a pool of blood. Although, in contrast to the madonna, this cast polyester sculpture was of the shadow realm, the two works still resembled one another. Both were evanescences of artificial artistic duration. In fact, each of Fritsch's works has the aura of a supernatural appearance, regardless of whether it is an elephant, a meticulously laid table, or a row of geometrically arranged candlesticks.

James Joyce took the epiphany—that moment in time in which the soul of a familiar object seems to shine out at us—as his point of departure for understanding art. Fritsch is also concerned with the essence of things. But whereas Joyce keeps to the prototype of Thomas Aquinas, the Düsseldorf artist develops precise mechanisms that give this old experience new meaning.

The aggressiveness of the Münster public response was certainly incited by the accentuated artificiality of the madonna figure. Fritsch cultivates the artificial in all of her works so that the plausibility of the natural becomes apparent for the first time. If the Münster madonna had been sandstone gray, she would more likely have been admired by the passers-by. Indeed, the cold, light-yellow varnish made it clear what the religious sculpture really was—plastic. Here is, perhaps, the true scandal of this sculpture. It combines the mystical uniqueness of the holy appearance, whose location and circumstances already impart a meaning, with the commercial realm of mass-produced merchandise. The madonna image, which leads one to expect the inspiration of a religious artist, really possesses no unique form at all. Rather, it is a duplicate of a duplicate. In this mass-produced article, religious cult competes with consumer cult.

Even the little madonna on the merchandise rack, the predecessor of the large-scale Münster Virgin, hints at a connection between art and consumerism. Still more important here, for Fritsch, was the exact presentation. The merchandise rack creates its own precisely defined space for the art objects. It is more an instrument of form than of theme. It forces the commodity aspect of artworks to stand out and endangers the epiphanic effect of a work in which the essence is shown. Yet in contrast to Haim Steinbach's or Jeff Koons's works, Fritsch's do not emphasize art as the circulation of consumer goods. The display of the objects, their mass production, which requires very specific materials, and finally even the purchase—all to be expected in a capitalistic society—have gone into Fritsch's works as medium. As such, her work has more to do with the self-evident recognition of working and of existential principles than with a critical message. (Indeed, no viewer may overlook the fact that this attitude of the artist again carries meaning itself.) In any case, the effect of the madonna on the Salzstrasse can also be explained in that the image, robbed of religious form, robbed of all meaning, was transformed into a mere appearance. Her similarity to merchandise even lends to daily life a kind of pseudoreligious aura and creates a contemplative space in which the epiphany can unfold its effect.

Katharina Fritsch has a preference for difficult projects. Her organization becomes part of the work. The relationship between the idea (which usually goes back to an earlier simple perception whose meaning persists in the memory) and the form of organization is that of a transformation. The imagination is objectivized in the process. Every object which so originates thus becomes a prototype.

The reader occasionally gets an idea of the effort involved in realizing the work by looking at the acknowledgments in the catalogs. In 1987 Fritsch exhibited a life-size green elephant in the Kaiser Wilhelm Museum in Krefeld. The acknowledgments on the last page of the little catalog reveal that permission had to be obtained from a natural history museum in which the stuffed original was located; the taxidermist there had to mold the form parts for the new cast himself with the help of assistants. A large studio had to be rented, where experts helped put the synthetic animal together. The research involved in finding the right materials, the design of

Elephant, 1987. Installation at Kaiser Wilhelm Museum, Krefeld polyester and wood, 12 ft 7 in. x 12 ft 4 in. x 5 ft 3 in. (4.2 x 3.8 x 1.6 m) Jablonka Galerie, Cologne

the supporting structure, and the development of methods also involved considerable time and the participation of numerous individuals. A recording of the monotonous dripping of water on leaves, *Regen (Rain)*, was not simply borrowed from a sound archive; Fritsch had in mind a certain bush that was supposed to lure the music out of the raindrops, and it took a while before she was finally able, one night, with the assistance of a sound man, to record it.

Eight Tables with Eight Objects, 1984, mixed media
Table: 29 x 187 in. overall (75 x 480 cm) Johnen & Schöttle, Cologne

Such laborious processes reveal what kind of precision Fritsch expects from the materialization of an idea. They also intimate a sensitivity for the process itself in which a concept is transformed into material. Along the laborious way from the idea to the finished object, the power of realization, a leitmotif for one's understanding of art, becomes all the more clear. For, without a doubt, this is where Fritsch's interest in art begins: ideal images which become real. Out of the paradoxical impact of ideal and contingency, she strikes the creative sparks of art.

By "idea" here I do not mean general, abstract ideas. The point of departure in Fritsch's work is usually an intimate biographical experience that has left its traces in the artist's imagination. And when she transforms such an ideal image into reality, it has something of that magic that has been connected with the work of the artist since antiquity. "I often choose objects that are loaded in themselves," Fritsch has said. "They should be autobiographical and of general significance at the same time in order to be comprehensible." The objects which are gathered together in the merchandise rack can also be understood as a kind of autobiographical text, as a collection of all those things from earlier times that have left their imprint on the imagination of the artist. This is as true of the madonna as it is of the elephant.

The epiphanic effect of this art unfolds itself in the play between the "specific" and the "general." Sometimes the "general," the essence of the thing, comes across more than the "specific," autobiographical experiences or fantasy. Then the specificity of the appearance of a madonna or a ghost takes precedence over the generality of an industrial product. It is seldom that industrial products play a role in Fritsch's work. Nonetheless, the transformation of the idea into an object always involves the development of a general production process. Each work is a prototype that could also be produced in series.

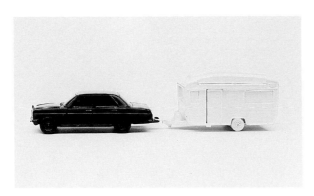

Black Car with White Housetrailer, 1979, sheet metal, plastic, varnish
9 3/4 x 2 1/2 x 2 in. (25 x 6 x 5 cm) Johnen & Schöttle, Cologne

Just how important the idea of the serial is for Fritsch can be seen most clearly in the piece *Company at Table*, which she exhibited in 1988 in the Kunsthalle in Basel. What we consider most individual, the individual human being, was repeated here thirty-one times, cast in polyester. The figures sat across from each other at a long table. A white tablecloth, printed with a red pattern, unified the scene, heightening the formal unity already present in the black and white painted figures. As is often the case, a similar motif can be found in an earlier work, Fritsch's 1986 *Round Black Table with Four Chairs* presented in the Cologne gallery Johnen & Schöttle. In it two identically clothed persons sat motionless across from each other at a table in the exact configuration that they are painted on the cups and plates in front of them. Here too, a serialization of the motif took place. The installation in Basel was implemented even more radically, like a double mirror in which the figures sitting opposite each other repeat endlessly in a long, virtual-image shaft.

This effect was reinforced by the endless repetition of the pattern on the tablecloth. Fritsch experienced it as a metaphor for circular thinking: "A pattern has no beginning and no end. It stands metaphorically for someone who 'thinks in circles.'" In her mail-order catalog of 1981 under Order No. 7, Fritsch offered a wallpaper design. The offer was accepted by a museum in 1985. For her installation, Fritsch painted the walls of a room in the pattern she had advertised. She was aiming neither at mural painting nor at decoration. Ornament as serial design is a strategy Fritsch uses to take the depth of meaning out of the work. Thus her serial work is aimed in the same direction as her work on the standards of consumerism: here, as there, she is concerned with a reduction of the semantics of artistic works, so that the essential can be experienced in the epiphany beyond all terminology.

Stephan Schmidt-Wulffen
(Translation: Katherine Funk-Roos)

Dark Green Tunnel, 1979
colored wax
3 1/4 x 3 1/4 x 31 1/4 in.
(8 x 8 x 80 cm)
Johnen & Schöttle, Cologne

Charms, 1986
wood, glass, chimney-sweep
stickers
Charms: 2 in. each (5 cm)
Jablonka Galerie, Cologne

*Side Table with Angel and
Bottle*, 1985
painted wood, plexiglas, zinc
foil (with wallpaper)
36 3/4 x 31 1/2 x 15 3/4 in.
(94 x 80 x 40 cm)
Galerie Daniel Buchholz,
Cologne

Candlesticks, 1985
steel, wax
62 1/2 x 47 x 47 in.
(160 x 120 x 120 cm)
Johnen & Schöttle, Cologne

Black Table with China, 1985
wood, plastic and paint
Overall: 35 1/2 x 59 x 59 in.
(90.17 x 149.86 x 149.86 cm)
Table: 29 1/4 x 39 in.
(75 x 100 cm)
Chair: 35 1/4 x 58 1/2 in. each
(90 x 150 cm)
Collection First Bank System,
Inc., Minneapolis

Elephant, 1987
Installation at Kaiser Wilhelm
Museum, Krefeld
polyester and wood
12 ft 7 in. x 12 ft 4 in. x 5 ft 3 in.
(4.2 x 3.8 x 1.6 m)
Jablonka Galerie, Cologne

Company at Table, 1988
polyester, wood and cotton
55 x 52 1/2 x 68 4/5 in.
(129.70 x 133.35 x 174.75 cm)
Jablonka Galerie, Cologne

Ghost and Pool of Blood, 1988
polyester resin, plexiglas
Ghost: 78 3/4 x 23 1/2 in.
(200 x 59.7 cm)
Blood: 21 x 82 1/2 in.
(53.5 x 209.6 cm)
Collection Ydessa Hendeles,
Courtesy Ydessa Hendeles Art
Foundation

ROBERT GOBER

Robert Gober's use of the room as a structuring motif for his presentation of sculpture goes back to 1978 and his small-scale replicas of nineteenth-century New England vernacular houses. The interiors of these three-by-three-foot houses were finished with minute details such as radiators, parquet floors, and wallpaper. In this context, the room emerges as a metaphorical structure linking the domestic or private with the political or social.

We begin to discern in Gober's early work, in what might be loosely described as its public sphere, references to a repressed history of America. One of the doll houses, for instance, presents an innocent Americana in the imagery of its wallpaper—block prints of the states of the nation. Another plays more forcefully with nationalist symbolism; split in two, with one half Southern plantation-style Greek Revival and the other half stripped of those stylistic features, it reveals the schizophrenic, master/slave roots of a vernacular style by suggesting the contradiction between the classic "purity" of white cultural aspirations, symbolized by the architecture of ancient Greece, and the fact of an American culture built on the economic and moral exploitation of race.

Installation Paula Cooper Gallery, New York, 1985. *Kaleidoscopic Sink*, 1985; *The Scary Sink*, 1985; *The Flying Sink*, 1985

From the outset, however, Gober has wed this level of public reference with a private, domestic narrative. The psychological dynamic in these early dollhouses worked itself out spatially. A potent expressivity was attached to the interior divisions and to the important divisions of inside and outside, underscoring the dimensions of exclusion, sexual difference, intimacy, and privacy that these divisions suggest. In later full-scale work, the room device successfully bridges the gaps between individual pieces of sculpture placed within it, allowing a mental landscape to materialize from the juxtaposition of objects in space.

The room motif emerged during roughly the same period that Gober exhibited his sinks and urinals in standard gallery exhibitions (1982-85). I want to suggest here that a sexual politics determined both the iconography and the mode of production of Gober's roomlike installations and individual sculptures. That Gober's work contained a gendered polemic (if that is not too strong a word) did not make it especially groundbreaking because, as feminists might argue, all images were the products and property of the male gaze, and nothing could make these works extraordinary. But the feminism of the late seventies already had challenged male gender assumptions, and gay men joined in the dialogue, specifically questioning the exclusivity of mainstream culture's definitions of masculinity. But Gober's sculpture and rooms take on a particular meaning in the context of the discourse shaped by the powerfully feminist art of, for instance, Barbara Kruger and Cindy Sherman.

Pair of Urinals, 1987
wood, wire lath, plaster, enamel
paint
21 1/2 x 15 1/4 x 15 3/4 in.
each
(54.6 x 38.7 x 40 cm)
Collection Frederik Roos,
Stockholm, Sweden

By 1986 the outlines of Gober's polemic had emerged in both the room installations and the sculpture. Gober's sink and urinal sculptures inaugurated a male narrative. The sinks, begun in 1982, appeared first as straightforward remakes of actual objects but began alluding more explicity to maleness when Gober began shaping their upper sections to vaguely resemble male torsos. The buried sinks bear powerful references to ghosts and to tombstones, suggesting his growing concern with sexuality in the age of AIDS.

At the same time, working with other artists, Gober created two influential roomlike installations in small galleries in downtown New York; his choice of collaborative production introduced another important aspect of gender signification into his work. In these installations Gober challenged the patriarchal model of artistic production, undermining the authority of the single "masterwork" created by the male artist working alone. Gober's alternative model for creativity affirmed the importance of male-male bonding, the family, and the worker's collective. That relationships were involved in the creative process underscored the transformation of the gallery into a personalized space.

The room installations to which I refer here began with a collaboration with Kevin Larmon at Nature Morte in March 1986. The installation combined two of Gober's sinks, two of Larmon's dark, shellacked still-life paintings on a surface of easily decomposable old newspapers, a headboard, and a seatless chair borrowed from an antique store. The found object in this installation, the headboard, was compelling formally as an abstracted shape and metaphorically. Its presence implied that the room was like an attic, storing a collection of remainders. In the headboard the idea of the bed as both neutral sculptural form and sexualized object entered Gober's sculptural lexicon of sinks and urinals, objects which suggest similar readings.

Following this exhibition, Gober orchestrated an installation for the Cable Gallery in September 1986 in which he also included the work of other artists: a cone-shaped mound of earth by Meg Webster, a painting of a fantastic landscape of merging bodies by Alan Turner, and a disparate accumulation of objects scattered on the wall by Nancy Shaver. Gober's own addition to this ensemble was a single bed, which he constructed. Gober's impetus for making this bed was his desire to turn from the illusionism of his sinks and urinals, which were plaster facsimiles of actual objects, to the minimalist gesture, as in the art of Carl Andre, of constructing the actual object itself (Gober's bed is, after all, a real, functional bed). Moreover, he wanted, I believe, to craft this concrete, functional object in the manner of the traditional household craftsman. This was carpenter's, not artist's, work, man's work for the home, not production for the marketplace.

Two Partially Buried Sinks,
1986-87
cast iron, enamel
24 x 72 x 2 3/4 in.
(60.7 x 182.9 x 7 cm)
Private collection, Connecticut

Robert Gober's studio, New York, 1987. *Two Urinals*, 1986; *Corner Bed*, 1986-87; *Distorted Playpen*, 1986

This iconographical reading is possible precisely because Gober conceived of the exhibition space not as a neutral container but as a space where a choreographed ensemble of objects made by and belonging to other people interacted. Similar to the installation at Nature Morte, this space and its objects had a domestic ambiance. Gober's decision to present a seemingly outdoor piece, Meg Webster's earth mound, indoors and to place it in relation to the simple bed gave this particular room a distinguishing surrealism or fantasy, an uncanny association with children's fairy tales. Illustrations of children's stories, such as Leslie Brooke's depiction of Goldilocks investigating the empty house of the three bears, or Maurice Sendack's portrayal of a child's nighttime hallucinations in *Where the Wild Things Are*, were images prompted by Gober's room at Cable. That the installation implies the memory of infancy was borne out by Gober's subsequent construction of the baby cribs and playpens as sculptures.

In the 1989 collaborative installation for the Institute of Contemporary Art, Boston, Gober completely fused room and installation by building an ideal

enclosed room within the neutral gallery space. Although he conceived the installation out of the simple image of a door closed then open, this image gradually evolved into an exploration of the oppositions of ideal and real, utopia and dystopia, and public and private in a series of other images related to American history, a subject he had addressed in the dollhouses. The artist meticulously fabricated a door and doorframe, and to emphasize the construct he disengaged the one from the other. The doorframe became a threshold, a portal privileging the viewer to pass from a rough exterior—unfinished walls revealing their primitive board and batten construction—to an interior of extreme delicacy and beauty—classic pale blue walls trimmed with cream-colored wooden moldings.

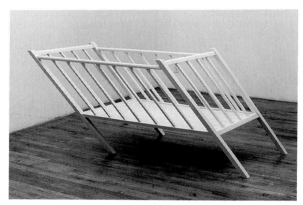

Pitched Crib, 1987, wood, enamel paint, 38 1/2 x 77 x 52 in. (97.8 x 195.6 x 132.1 cm) Dakis Joannou, Athens

Gober orchestrated the edenic interior from a spare ensemble of objects: a low bed of compacted earth covered by a quilt of living moss by Meg Webster dominated the center of the room; opposite the doorframe and leaning against the wall was the door that Gober had constructed; the remaining facing walls each displayed a painting—Albert Bierstadt's nineteenth-century painting of Lake Tahoe opposite Richard Prince's handwritten laconic, almost vernacular American slang joke about a drunk fireman. Prince's joke, which was meant to question the authenticity of the experiences embodied by the objects, nevertheless did not undercut the powerful utopian effect of the pastoral bed in the ideal room. Webster's bed, framed by the open door and at the center of the room, introduced an image of sexual and domestic intimacy and coupled it with the characteristically American theme of nature as idyll.

Playpen, 1987
wood, enamel paint
26 1/8 x 39 x 39 in.
(66.3 x 99.1 x 99.1 cm)
Saatchi Collection, London

The room for this exhibition at the Newport Harbor Art Museum, like the rooms for the Paula Cooper Gallery in the Fall of 1989, Gober has created without the collaboration of others. As such, I think we should construe these independent installations as complex individual works of sculpture. Both the container and the contained exist as striking sculptural metaphors for complex intellectual processes. Like the earlier works, the newer rooms are chambers of the mind which fuse narratives of private experience with social-sexual politics. The room at the Newport Harbor Art Museum alludes to sleep and infancy in the whitewashed replica of a child's crib—a straightforward facsimile of a standard element of childhood. Here also we find the door and the doorframe, with their specific relationship interrupted by the door's display as an independent sculpture in the room. The minimalist sculptural presence of the door is echoed by one of Gober's most enigmatic pieces, *Plywood*, which appears to be just that—a piece of plywood—and nothing more. Yet Gober has meticulously fabricated the plywood, layer by layer, in an obsessive desire to wrest identity from an archetypal process of industrial production. If one is unaware of its process, this object is virtually mute. It resists interpretation: for most people who see it, it is insufferably—and powerfully—dumb.

Before trying to suggest an analysis of Gober's brilliant choice of images in his *Hanging Man/Sleeping Man* wallpaper for the room, we should simply note its more explicit reference to the human body. Observers of Gober's work have remarked on the absence or the loss of the body in his oeuvre. Quite literally, the human body (and in the case of Gober's dog bed and recent kitty-litter bags, the bodies of domesticated animals) is absent. Yet Gober's sculptural objects (a crib, a chair, a bed, a urinal) have always been surrogates for the body or empty receptacles for it. In later work, Gober has simply introduced a more explicit representation of human form: the hunter on the fabric covering the cushion of his dog bed; the photograph of the dress in his installation at Gallery 303 with Christopher Wool; the spectral wedding dress, molded around a mannequin, but standing empty of a body in his recent installation at Paula Cooper; and the representations of male and female genitalia and the hanging man/sleeping man motifs of his wallpaper.

Corner Bed, 1986-87
wood, cotton, enamel paint
44 x 77 x 41 1/2 in.
(111.8 x 195.6 x 105.4 cm)
Galerie Jean Bernier, Athens

Installation at Institute of Contemporary Art, Boston, 1988. Gober's door from *Untitled (Door and Doorframe)*, 1987-88; Albert Bierstadt *Lake Tahoe, California*, 1867; Meg Webster *Moss Bed*, 1986-88

Gober's choice of images is mysterious. How images enter his lexicon is never completely clear, but once there they seem impressive natural additions to his vocabulary. The *Hanging Man/Sleeping Man* wallpaper covering the room constructed for the Newport Harbor Art Museum portrays a white man sleeping obliviously through the racist lynching of a black man. The sleeping man was suggested by a Macy's ad, the lynched man by the racism that has recently riddled New York. Gober's juxtaposition of these two images surely suggests the arrogance of patriarchal white male indifference to the oppression of black men in America and the relationship of racism to repressive sexual morality.

Intentionally or not, Gober has presented a juxtaposition of images—sleeping white man/lynched black man—that fits a complex argument advanced by American black women intellectuals in the early twentieth century and recently brought to light by Hazel Carby. This argument places lynching at the core of an analysis of the relation between white terrorism, economic oppression, and codes of sexuality. Carby quotes the black writer Pauline Hopkins as saying in 1900 that "lynching was instituted to crush the manhood of the enfranchised black."

Hopkins' argument, which was built on the writing of another black woman of her era, Ida B. Wells, was that after emancipation, the white population lost control over the bodies of blacks, who were no longer slaves. In order to reestablish control, whites invented the crime of rape of white women by black men. (Statistics do not prove that white women of the South were to any significant extent so victimized.) The fabrication of a sexual crime made lynching permissible. Afterward, lynching for any crime was possible.

Though Gober may or may not be aware of this historical argument, much more rich in issues of patriarchy, emasculation, and their relation to political and economic conditions than I can discuss here, it is not remote from the concerns of his own art and politics. Marginalization, victimization, death, the centrality of issues of gender and sexuality to political situations, and the recounting of such a history by a marginalized group (black women writers) are all elements that explode from the images that people Gober's rooms. By intuitively making such connections in the wallpaper imagery of his latest room, Gober links the present public concerns of his art with his earlier domestic ones— his interest in craft, in childhood, as exemplified by the nursery, and in collaborative work. In continuously making more explicit those themes that had been implicit in his earlier works, Gober has expanded his visual lexicon in a way that helps reveal the social dimensions of private experience.

Elisabeth Sussman

Untitled (door and doorframe),
1987-88
Installation at Institute of Contemporary Art, Boston, with
Meg Webster *Moss Bed*,
1986-88
mixed media
Door: 84 x 34 x 1 1/2 in.
(213.4 x 86.4 x 3.8 cm)
Doorframe: 90 x 43 x 5 1/2 in.
(228.6 x 109.2 x 14 cm)
Private collection

Untitled, 1988
wood, steel, enamel paint
30 x 32 x 59 in.
(76.2 x 81.3 x 149.9 cm)
Saatchi Collection, London

Untitled (door and doorframe),
1987-88
Installation at Paula Cooper
Gallery, New York, 1989
mixed media
Door: 84 x 34 x 1 1/2 in.
(213.4 x 86.4 x 3.8 cm)
Doorframe: 90 x 43 x 5 1/2 in.
(228.6 X 109.2 X 14 cm)
Private collection

Untitled (dog bed), 1987
handwoven rattan, cotton flannel,
fabric paint
11 x 38 x 30 in.
(27.9 x 96.5 x 76.2 cm)
Private collection, New York

Plywood, 1987
laminated fir
95 1/4 x 46 1/2 x 5/8 in.
(241.9 x 118.1 x 1.6 cm)
Collection Andrew Ong,
Courtesy Paula Cooper Gallery

Installation at Paula Cooper
Gallery, New York, 1989
Wedding Gown, 1989; *Cat Litter*,
1989; *Hanging Man/Sleeping
Man*, 1989

Untitled, 1988
textile paint on cotton flannel
27 1/2 x 34 1/4 in.
(70 x 87.6 cm)
Galerie Gisela Capitain, Cologne

Opposite:
Installation at Paula Cooper
Gallery, New York, 1989.
Wedding Gown, 1989; *Hanging
Man/Sleeping Man*, 1989

JEFF KOONS

Jeff Koons's stainless steel statues in this exhibition represent one phase in an astonishing career that I will address in general terms with special emphasis on the ceramic and wood statuary with which Koons has sharply altered the outlook for contemporary art. Koons's recent work, besides being innovative as sculpture, demonstrates present cultural change more convincingly than any critical description and more intelligibly than any theoretical model, incidentally occasioning the pleasure that always attends art's power to figure forth truth. Many people dislike it, but what bothers them is less the work, I think, than the particular, direly soulless truth it brings into focus. In effect, they blame the messenger for the message. Such a response does not befit a serious consideration of art, though its meanings—as, like the work, testifying cultural data—demand respect. Revulsion against an artistic phenomenon is sometimes at least as instructive as enthusiasm for it. Revulsion may be a positive oracle in the strange, consequential instance of Jeff Koons.

For a philosophical statement keyed to the implications of Koons's art, I propose this: *There are no longer any subjects, only objects.* The proposition is absurd. It is pronounced unbelievable by the mere fact that an "I" proposes it, "I" being the proper name of the subjective and the grammatical proof of a subject's existence ("I" is, therefore I am). But absurdity seems the cardinal point of Koonsism, imposing a cartoonish aspect on any presumption to the dignity of the subjective within its field. Koonsism doesn't make fools of people, exactly; rather, it casts fools and people as the same thing. This is the vision always cultivated by caricature, the derisive treatment of subjectivity as an objective "sight." Caricature is often noted as a special feature of present culture (with particular richness in the art and writing of Mike Kelley). What's unique about Koons is his radical extension of the caricatural impulse to a point where derision disappears because no imaginable subject remains to be superior to what is derided. There is no one to be in on the joke with, unless it is a Kafkaesque, unsympathetic deity.

Koons is at one with a blanketing absurdity characteristic of this historical moment whose central event is the end of the Cold War. Like other postwar periods in our century that gave rise to the absurdity-obsessed movements of dadaism and existentialism, the present is marked by a bleak giddiness in the absence of any credible value except, in our case, the triumphal capitalist imperatives of economic growth and mass-cultural homogenization—paradigms represented in hallucinatory caricature by Koons. No assertion of value seems quite real today unless related to a "market." At a time when communist nations practically hanker for our malaise, ideological opposition to the tyranny of money becomes impotent, and populist resistance, if any, swings to the fundamentalist right. Thus do the failures of materialism (consumerist and "dialectical" alike) to humanize society seem inescapable malignancies of nature, congenital deformations to be suffered in anxious or hilarious awe and with the sort of free-floating discontent that makes people talk back to their television sets.

Koons's art caricatures Art, the Commodity Supreme. His public uses of his own persona caricature The Artist. The viewing situations he directs turn the viewer (you, me) into a caricature of The Viewer—The Appreciative Viewer, if one likes the work, or The Hostile Viewer, if one doesn't. The Indifferent Viewer of Koons's work is hard to conceive, unless as a passive-aggressive Hostile. Koons's equanimity in the face of no matter what response apotheosizes the press agent's credo, There Is No Such Thing as Bad Publicity, steamrollering the moral dimension of discourse to a paper-thin silhouette. His way of talking about his enterprise in terms of a "responsibility" of the artist to "seduce and manipulate" is at once fatuous and irrefutable, a dopey position that happens to fit the contemporary facts. Koons doesn't insult critical intelligence, because tacitly ready to grant its own license to seduce and manipulate, with the gray fireworks that pass for ideas in the art magazines. He doesn't subvert the promotional structures of the art game, because intent

Louis (XIV), 1986
stainless steel
46 x 27 x 15 in.
(116.8 x 68.5 x 38.1 cm)
Collection of the artist,
Courtesy Sonnabend Gallery

on displaying them with the thrilling click-clack of outsized Transformer toys. He is not ironic. He is a cartoon artist of cartoon art in a cartoon cosmos with a cartoon cast of thousands. Welcome to the real world of the nineties.

What makes Koons important, and not just an opportunistic symptom of deranged times, is the superlative quality of his art as sculpture, becoming a legitimate heir to some of the strongest esthetic comprehensions of recent decades. All the attractions and repulsions that can be associated with him are clearly ordered, like iron filings by a magnet, in the presence of his work. His sculptural mode is essentially minimalist: outer-directed, irradiating the viewer's physical and psychological space. His innovation is to transpose the standard push-pull of minimalism—cold geometry in tension with surface warmth à la Andre, Flavin, Judd, et al.—to a purely psychological plane of alienated content versus irresistible form (another pretty good definition of caricature). The result, as with minimalism, is an instantaneous clarifying of the viewing situation, but to an extent far richer than minimalism's taciturn revelation of "art space." Koons's objects differentiate their settings not just materially as sites continuous with the physical world, but culturally as places of ritualized consumption in a totally mediated society.

While determinedly stone dead at the level of "expression," which Koons scorns as completely as any poststructuralist theorist, his recent works broadcast the news that energy exists somewhere and somehow, and perhaps everywhere in every way, without being available to anyone in particular. The work exalts ramifications of sensibility while amputating sensibility's roots in both reason and emotion. "Objects live," the statues as much as say, "and everything alive is an object." Looking at them, I flounder in pleasure—pleasure defined as perception of energy—that has nothing to do with me. The stridently "happy" images of the ceramic and wood sculptures—the perky Popples and simpering animal lovers, the sniggery nudes—seem to me naked faces of schizophrenic misery: joyless joy, mirthless

Popples, 1988, porcelain (Ed. 3), 29 1/2 x 23 x 12 in. (74.9 x 58.4 x 30.5 cm) Sonnabend Gallery, New York, and Donald Young Gallery, Chicago

mirth, and, all in all, "darkness visible," in Milton's phrase for the atmospherics of Hell. Koons is a theologian of culture without individuals.

The development of Koons's art since one of its earliest motifs, that of his vacuum-cleaner displays of the early eighties, can scarcely be termed "growth," given the antiorganic thrust of Koonsism. It is more akin to the mechanical refinement of style in any fashion-driven industry, such as pop music, taken to a spooky extreme. (It's no accident that Koons has been preoccupied with Michael Jackson, whose machine-likeness extends to treating his own face and body virtually as modifiable systems of communications technology: Koons and Jackson

Italian Woman, 1986
stainless steel
30 x 18 x 11 in.
(76.2 x 45.7 x 27.9 cm)
Collection Leo Castelli

are the same kind of artist.) At first, Koons was content to work with existing conventions. His vacuum-cleaner pieces put pop items in minimalist boxes, as it were, with a conceptual logic hinting at simple eccentricity: spotless cleaning equipment in airtight containment suggests a monument to a cleanliness compulsion. But already this work shows a startling decisiveness and an air of wide-open mystery, of hiding in plain sight, reminiscent of no other artist.

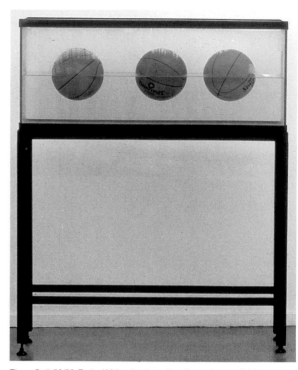

Three Ball 50/50 Tank, 1985, mixed media, dimensions variable, Sonnabend Gallery, New York

American black culture, and whatever else you can make of them—in a physically "impossible" way. All sorts of analytical riffs propose themselves: reflecting on the nature of an object in pictorial space, say, or on the quasi-holographic zone of estheticized space created by a sculptural pedestal. (Koons was about to reclaim the pedestal for a medium that has been wandering around on the floor, with diminishing returns, since David Smith in the 1950s.) The tanks can easily be read as a synthesis of the Duchampian readymade, the minimalist theater of objecthood, and the Warholian iconization of commodities. The only thing conceivably wrong with them, indeed, may be a fairly insufferable surfeit of cleverness.

New Shelton Wet/Dry Double Decker, 1981, mixed media, dimensions variable, Sonnabend Gallery, New York

Koons's first truly major works were the singularly brilliant "equilibrium tanks," which literalize "art space" as a liquid. The liquid looks like water but suspends basketballs—which, thus hypersensitized, beam a symbolism of play, geometry, sexuality,

French Coach Couple, 1986
stainless steel
17 x 15 1/2 x 11 3/4 in.
(43.2 x 39.4 x 29.8 cm)
Private collection, Courtesy of
Sonnabend Gallery

The works by Koons in this show mark the transition, around 1986, toward the flawless power of the ceramic and wood sculptures: ten cast stainless-steel statues, each apostrophizing a specific, generically petit-bourgeois order of whimsy. While including one of the most perfectly delightful of modern art objects, *Rabbit*, these are minor works at the level of impact. Their conceptual mechanism is a bare two-step transposition of kitsch "originals" into fine-art "copies." Their significant feature is the caricature of motifs (often with a fine-art ancestry) that were caricatures to begin with, evoking the overdetermined, collective unconscious of ragamuffin historical and social cohorts. To look at this work is to participate in hapless mentalities that could swoon at Louis XIV's curly wig or chuckle at Bob Hope's "ski-jump nose." A sense of cold empathy with deprived classes is reinforced by the use of stainless steel, which (Koons has noted in interviews) might be called the platinum of poor people. The metal's literal reflectiveness reveals another objectified subject of the work: yourself, the probably upper-middle-class viewer.

Koons's ceramic and wood statuary does a lot more than just heighten the caricatural charge and visual glamour of the stainless-steel pieces. It kicks the dynamic of those pieces up to the full scale of their implication in a market-oriented art world, to a point where the raw facts of the work's commercial success become inextricable from its meaning as art. In editions of three that were shown simultaneously in 1988 in New York, Chicago, and Cologne, these works grossed seven million dollars, according to Koons. How seamless is the relation of the statues' attractive-repulsive magic and the art market's culture-climbing desire and supply-and-demand mechanics? So seamless, I suggest, that collectors didn't buy this work necessarily because they liked it or for any rational reason of investment or cachet. They bought it because its hypnotic poeticizing of the phenomenology of all markets made it less a product for sale than a hostage for ransom. Collectors had seven million dollars, galleries had the statues, and the exchange of one for the other was not optional. I think the swap was historic, an event to tell our grandchildren about: one of those days when twentieth-century absurdity went through the roof.

The new absurd of which Koons is the material philosopher is the old absurd of caricature, only universalized. Its general effect is that of any human activity observed without consideration of the activity's inner impulsion or outward purpose. Viewed with a sufficiently innocent eye, people walking down a street can appear as bizarre and disquieting as insects in closeup. For obvious reasons, we do not often permit ourselves, as individuals, this sanity-risking mode of observation. On the plane of mass culture, however, isn't it the essence of the ironic or, more usually, merely facetious detachment that regulates our collective world-view? Think of the confiding, dumb little smirk that every news anchorperson tosses periodically to the glass eye of the television camera. "We're immune to all this, right?" seems the smirk's gist. Some of us cling to art as a refuge in seriousness from the toxic stagnation of such immunity. We would not like to see art in the guise of insect behavior. That Koons shows art in precisely that guise explains the revulsion he triggers. But his undeniable cogency reminds us of something we are apt to forget: True seriousness is never a refuge from anything, but is a quality of courage in face of the least welcome truths. He also provides a vivid reference point for understanding what we are up against: himself (whoever that is), the major artist our all-conquering culture has deserved.

Peter Schjeldahl

Flowers, 1986
stainless steel
12 1/2 x 18 x 12 in.
(31.7 x 45.7 x 30.5 cm)
Collection Barbara and
Richard S. Lane

Two Kids, 1986
stainless steel
23 x 14 1/4 x 14 1/4 in.
(58.4 x 36.2 x 36.2 cm)
Collection Mera and Donald
Rubell

Doctor's Delight, 1986
stainless steel
11 x 6 3/4 x 5 3/4 in.
(27.9 x 17.1 x 14.6 cm)
Sonnabend Gallery, New York

Cape Codder Troll, 1986
stainless steel
21 x 8 1/2 x 9 in.
(53.3 x 21.6 x 22.9 cm)
Collection Robert and Honey
Dootson

Mermaid Troll, 1986
stainless steel
20 1/2 x 8 1/2 x 8 1/2 in.
(52.1 x 21.6 x 21.6 cm)
Collection of the artist,
Courtesy Sonnabend Gallery,
New York

Rabbit, 1986
stainless steel
41 x 19 x 12 in.
(104.1 x 48.3 x 30.5 cm)
Private collection

ANNETTE LEMIEUX

BOOKS AND THINGS

For the past four hundred or so years, Western culture has been literally shaped by the printed word. Our philosophies and world views, our concepts of truth and religion, our educational values and our general information, have all been fostered primarily through the printed press. The sources of our information about the world, the form that information takes, the speed and quality of its formation, its symbolic signification, and the context within which we have experienced the information have all combined to provide us with a perceptual framework within which to operate effectively both physically and psychologically.

Significantly, too, half of that period was devoted to the burgeoning of the industrial era which characterized itself through the production of mass-produced objects. The consumer object became a symbol by which people defined the degree to which they belonged to and were accepted by the culture.

That era has all but vanished. Not completely, of course. Changes as vast as these are always gradual. Books are still available (even read) and mass-produced; objects are still the focus of our materialist culture.

But now, without a doubt, we are in a new age: the age of the televisual. And it is television rather than the printed word that is shaping our cultural reality. As Neil Postman, author of *Amusing Ourselves to Death*, has observed:

> To put it plainly, television is the command center of the new epistemology. There is no audience so young that it is barred from television. There is no poverty so abject that it must forgo television. There is no education so exalted that it is not modified by television. And most important of all, there is no subject of public interest— politics, news, education, religion, science, sports—that does not find its way to television. Which means that all public understanding of these subjects is shaped by the biases of television.[1]

This is not a condemnation of television. For while the new televisual culture has transformed many familiar facets of our cultural life, it has also created positive structures to propel us into the twenty-first century. The televisual is simply our new reality. No more and no less. It is the new space we inhabit: a space of multiple screens and invisible electronic devices.

We have yet to understand fully the impact on our senses and on our psyches of this new cultural landscape where the primary relationship is the interface between us and the ubiquity of the screen. What is certain though is that we have reached a juncture, a crucial moment in history in which everything is being called into question. Our world is now a world of newer and faster technologies, technologies that threaten to accelerate our senses of time and space far beyond anything we have ever experienced before.

It is within this context that I would like to discuss Annette Lemieux's art. In contrast to many of her contemporaries, her work seems to confront *directly* this schism, this period in history when we seem to be at the crossroads of a new culture, a time in which we seem to have one foot in the old world and the other firmly planted in the new.

Showing Ones Colors, 1986
frames, glass, oil paint
22 x 16 1/2 in. each
(55.9 x 41.9 cm)
Collection Garry A. Weber,
Dallas

The work has often been described, mistakenly, as nostalgic, perhaps because of the objects she chooses to use in fabricating her oeuvre: second-hand books, outmoded frames, used furniture, antiquated globes, old photographs, timeworn sheet music, obsolete-looking typewriters, etc. But if these objects belong to another world, it is not to the smaller, simpler world of nostalgic recollection.

Lemieux's assemblages are like specters of a lost world of objects, ghostlike fragments of a forgotten order. They are arranged as though in pursuit of some lost harmony to the world. Each object looks as if it has been left behind by the integrated circuits of electronic function that reduce everything to the spacelessness of the screen.

A vintage typewriter, not a brand new word processor, is the focal point of *Oh, Promise Me*. Her chosen objects interface with the electronic world. We perceive these objects like mystic shells of an older, mechanistic culture. The power of Lemieux's work lies in her ability to see the mysterious interaction between the form and function of each object. She focuses on the impenetrability of lost design intentions, the forgotten connotations of "old" objects, and the lost origins of their former life.

Interestingly, many of the objects Lemieux gravitates toward are shell-like. The World War II helmets used in *The Seat of Intellect* or in *Party Hat* look like turtle shells. The oval picture frames of *Showing One's Colors* or the picture frame used in *Vacancy* resemble empty shells. She uses globes (e.g., *Geographics of the Sublime*) or round tables (e.g., *Preservation*). Roundness clearly fascinates Lemieux.

Symbolically, roundness (the circle) represents unity, continuity. Frozen in the prenatal egg form of their roundness, the swollen "ovaloids" of the family picture frame—painted, vacated, and made to resemble exotic eggs—in works like *Vacancy* or *Showing One's Colors* remind us of the amount of time we, as a culture, still invest in the ghost images of the past.

For Lemieux, the circle, the egg shape, the globe, and the dot seem to be evocations of history. Or, rather, of a *pre*history in an electronic era—a prehistory that no longer aspires to the kind of unity (roundness) which characterized the mechanistic universe we are leaving behind.

Adrift as we all are in this fast-changing culture, this is not a world for which Lemieux nostalgically yearns or even tries to revive. What her art does is to compel us to confront this world of objects as mysterious within the framework of the awakening new world of electronic communications. Lemieux's spaces are like old houses, vacated spheres. Like empty nests, they touch the heart of our own lost "home" of familiar, cultural touchstones.

The Seat of the Intellect, 1984
metal helmet, oil paint
11 x 9 7/16 x 6 1/2 in.
(29 x 24 x 16.5 cm)
Collection of the artist,
Courtesy Josh Baer Gallery

But her sometimes irreverent, jokey "misuse" of these objects is not at all a nostalgic reminiscence of these fractured spaces of perception. When two worlds collide, as they do at this historical moment, Lemieux perceives the juxtaposition of these familiar objects as tenuous connections, provisional tableaux of elements that exist shakily. They cohabit with the uneasy indifference of a bad marriage, soon to be irrevocably divorced.

Lemieux uses the arid, empty space of the museum or gallery like a desert backdrop for these fragments of the ruins of an industrial era. The gallery becomes a neutral space of interchangeability, a space which constitutes a different vision every few weeks. In this respect the work reflects, quite graphically, the nature of our constantly changing new culture where familiar objects take on new forms daily. Spatial interchangeability: this is the *real* object of Lemieux's work. It is a space that absorbs and drains everyday objects of their well-worn meanings. And yet, as much as they have been removed from the sphere of daily life, they continue to connote, to implicate us in a different vision.

In the 1960s Robert Rauschenberg and Jasper Johns used objects in their art as traces of the surrounding world. Utilizing commonplace objects in art gave the impression that the paintings belonged to the world of objects. The pursuit of the object in sixties assemblage seemed to suggest a reassuring proximity of the physical world to the world of art. It made paintings more *real*. This was an American sentiment—a desire to mingle with the democratic world of objects. It helped the works belong to a "family" of objects.

By contrast, a quarter of a century later, one could not find a more radically opposite position from Rauschenberg's and Johns's than Lemieux's. The elements of her work are no longer grounded in the unity of the everyday. Her objects are disturbingly withdrawn. They seem *un*real. Like absences or fragments of a missing clue, they are shells of the physical and the psychological.

Lemieux's objects are removed from the world within which they once functioned. They are placeless. And it is this very sense of placelessness that the art works explore. For in a televisual culture like ours, time and space—our normal channels of consciousness—are constantly shifting with the arbitrariness of a dreamscape. The ground of the "commonplace" has been pulled from beneath us. And the sense of intimacy with which everyday objects provided us in the sixties has been replaced in the eighties by distance, separation, withdrawal. The provisional resting place of the objects in the spaceless world of the exhibition space (and, by extension, of our new culture) becomes a mirror to the sense of impermanence that Lemieux's work evokes. Her pieces are like tableaux awaiting some essential component, something that has been lost forever to the surrounding space of time (history). They are like evasive clues which, in their combination, can perhaps jog the collective memory into recognition.

It's a Wonderful Life, 1986
oil on canvas, press type on
globe, wood stand
Canvas: 78 x 102 in.
(198.1 x 259.1 cm)
Globe and stand:
52 x 15 x 15 in.
(132.1 x 38.1 x 38.1 cm)
Collection Brooke and Carolyn
Alexander, New York

There is a silence that veils all Lemieux's works. The arrangements are mute. The world of sheet music, the books, or the literal world of the globes are all closed off from one another. There seems to be no point of interaction between them, only an endless meeting, like the cloverleafed intersections of freeways.

In the closing years of a historical era shaped by the printed word, it comes as no surprise that the book is a significant and recurring element in Lemieux's art. Like everything else in her work, the books are *used*. Nothing makes one more aware of something that has been used up than a book. More than any other object, it is vacated. Where the new book is brimful of possibilities, a used book is like a repository of lost and forgotten dreams. It is an abandoned world. Or, worse, a "non-world" waiting to be opened up. Books where a globe should be (in *Above and Below*)—why does the work make one think of eating? teeth? a broken circle? a division replacing wholeness? The unity of the book is a divisive one because it is subject to the either/or of the turned page. In this powerful work, the temporal unity of the book is juxtaposed with the implied absence of the spatial unity of the globe. Since reading is a subjection to the linearity of time, the books in the work begin to suggest a loss of space, an absence of the world, and an escape into

Installation at Wadsworth Atheneum, Hartford, 1988

another unseen, invisible world. The power of the work comes from its transformation of a seismic, historical moment into a single image. In *Above and Below*, the absented world of unity seems eroded, eaten into by the sequence of pages and books. The juxtaposition of presence and absence is eerie. It has a pathos which far transcends that of its components.

The cosmological is evoked in another book sculpture entitled *Domino Theory*. Brought down to the level of a children's game, the cosmos seems to be conspicuously absent. The books begin to resemble alternatives to the world. They become material absences, absent ghosts that inhabit the work.

In these works, Lemieux's found objects become memorabilia of a universalized past. Are we meant to take the works as allegories? the world as a pile of accidental thoughts? With Lemieux, we are never sure. We are returned to the reverberations of half-suggested possibilities. The very title *Above and Below* reduces heaven and hell to a simple spatial metaphor, bringing us into confrontation with the paucity of our world views.

Formal Wear, 1987
bronze (Ed. 9)
9 3/4 x 69 1/4 x 23 1/4 in.
(24.8 x 175.9 x 59.1 cm)
Collection Eli and Edythe L. Broad

Faced with the mystery of contemporary, cosmological thinking, Lemieux's art evokes the pathos of the impossibility of art's muteness in the face of science's absolutes. We are trapped in Lemieux's work, locked within the limits of representation. Like a psychological claustrophobia, we are forced to use her models rather in the way Wittgenstein saw his early philosophy—as a ladder to be kicked away once climbed. Just as Wittgenstein's early philosophy is only communicable beyond the limits of language—in the unsayable—so Lemieux's work can only be grasped in what is absent, invisible.

The book sculptures are like toppled tombstones (*Tall Tales*), stacked and barred from use like the junk of a postliterate age. Closed, empty worlds, they are old containers like Lemieux's other chosen objects. We begin to see the books as part of an assembly of the dead in a culture of forgetfulness. There is neither a sense of reanimation of these objects to a second life nor any sense of recovery to a former life of use. It is as if their past has been forgotten. They are objects of a cultural amnesia from a world of forgotten origins.

Lemieux's art functions like a poetry of "misrecognition." The intimacy which is aroused when we look at objects that still contain traces of their former use is counterposed by a distance permeated by an aura of death in these objects that are displaced in the museum or gallery space.

In a culture in which the physical order of the commonplace is being replaced with the ordered sequence of signs and functions (the technological), a culture whose family of objects is being eroded, disappearing into the multifunctionality of the electronic network, sculpture is an act of resistance and defiance. Or else, as in Lemieux's case, it is a confrontation with the void that lies at the heart of the mass-produced object and which becomes the central vortex of an electronic dissolution of the object in today's world.

Rosetta Brooks

NOTE

1. Neil Postman. *Amusing Ourselves to Death* (New York: Penguin, 1985), p. 78.

Sonnet, 1987
wood shelf, books, wood frame
50 x 33 x 5 1/2 in.
(127 x 83.8 x 14 cm)
Collection of the artist,
Courtesy Josh Baer Gallery

Opposite:
Oh, Promise Me, 1985
Royal typewriter, table, player
piano music roll
Scroll: 16 ft (5 meters)
maximum
Typewriter: 12 x 16 x 14 in.
(30.5 x 40.6 x 38.1 cm)
Private collection, Switzerland

Left:
Detail from
Oh, Promise Me
Royal typewriter with altered
keys

Tall Tale, 1987
78 books, wood bookshelf,
66 x 10 1/2 x 8 1/4 in.
(167.6 x 26.7 x 21 cm)
Private collection, Los Angeles

Two Short Stories, 1987
books, text
Left: 18 x 9 3/4 x 6 1/2 in.
(45.7 x 24.7 x 16.5 cm)
Right: 19 x 10 x 7 3/4 in.
(48.3 x 25.4 x 19.7 cm)
Collection of the artist,
Courtesy Josh Baer Gallery

Above and Below, 1988
metal globe stand, books
44 x 61 1/4 x 31 in.
(111.7 x 155.6 x 78.7 cm)
Collection Anne and William
Hokin, Chicago

Domino Theory, 1988
used books
6 1/2 x 70 x 65 in.
(16.5 x 177.8 x 165.1 cm)
Courtesy Studio Guenzani,
Milano

Molding Minds, 1988
metal and plaster objects, wood
pedestal
41 1/2 x 48 x 16 in.
(105.4 x 121.9 x 40.6 cm)
Collection Ronnie and Samuel
Heyman, New York

Preservation, 1988
velvet cushion, wood table,
sheet music, resin
26 1/2 x 24 1/4 in.
(67.3 x 61.6 cm)
Collection Alice and Marvin
Kosmin, Courtesy Josh Baer
Gallery

JUAN MUÑOZ

Juan Muñoz's first one-person exhibition in Madrid
in 1984 included several small iron balconies. Each
was anchored to a large round column by means of
four lanky legs. The balconies were accompanied
by floor-bound iron structures resembling towers
built on rather tenuous stilts. As if a mutinous corps
of spindly legs had inched up the sides of the
columns, angling in just enough to keep their cargo
level, the balconies elevated and mobilized the spatial
and narrative orientation of the viewer. They drew
the viewer into a drama of watching and waiting.

The sculptural lookouts were grouped together
under the title of *General Miaja Looking for the
Guadiana River*. General Miaja, an anti-Francoist
leader, defended Madrid during the final days of the
Spanish Civil War. The search referred to the elusive
path of a river whose course flowed both above and
below ground.[1] Metaphorically, the balconies alluded
to an uncertain and potentially unfulfillable quest.
They pursued what may seem visible or knowable
but in reality is not.

Muñoz's balconies soon grew in scale and finesse
and established a direct relationship with the wall.
Their leggy supports gradually disappeared, reduc-
ing structural and formalistic interference to a
minimum. *London Balcony* (1987) juts dramatically
from the plane of the wall. It is a curved platform
whose railing flattens out on either side and continues for a short distance along the face of the wall.
The conspicuously vacant structure appears as an
apparition, an evocation pressed into physical form.
It is ripe with connotations of nineteenth-century
romanticism. One's memory does not have to venture
far to recall the early veiled majas that Francisco
Goya positioned behind balcony railings. Edouard
Manet readapted the locale in *The Balcony*
(1868-69), transforming it into a stage set for
attitudes of detachment and alienation of the
French bourgeoisie. Although Muñoz's balcony is
figureless, it implies the vacant gazes and private
reveries that Manet's players pictured. Muñoz has
defined a zone inhabited by utter inactivity; yet it is
the very absence of specific circumstantial evidence
that enables the viewer to activate the situation.
The potential for narrative is locked in the viewer's

London Balcony, 1987, iron, 25 3/4 x 39 x 16 in. (66 x 100 x 41 cm)
Private collection, London

imagination rather than in the physical form of the
sculpture.

The vacant form, in fact, surreptitiously acts to lure
the unwitting viewer into a cat and mouse game
negotiated between the observer and the observed.
The player walks in front of and below the perch
watching the "other"—the imaginary one(s) who
would occupy the balcony—while the "other" turns
the watching on the walker. Walking becomes inte-
grally bound to viewing and perceiving. It is an
activity inherently suggestive of transit and of
search, one that exerts considerable weight in
Muñoz's sculpture.

Balcony with Floor, 1987
iron, wood, paint
dimensions variable
Galería Marga Paz, Madrid

The artist has allowed various objects such as staircases, floors, and banisters, in addition to balconies, to imply physical and metaphorical passage. Muñoz's *Banister* (1986) undeniably references the function and simple elegance of the utilitarian object. However, its noble isolation and its lack of narrative confirmation transform the obvious into the enigmatic. Muñoz's handrail offers a tangible moment of rest and guidance in an otherwise blind journey. In *Favorite Banister* (1988) an inordinately long handrail is interrupted by a whimsical bridge of iron grillwork. As with each object/protagonist in his work, Muñoz subjected the banister to multiple formal and situational variations, until its evocative potential exhausted itself.[2]

The Banister, 1986, wood, 5 1/2 x 78 x 6 1/4 in. (200 x 14 x 16 cm)
Galería Marga Paz, Madrid

One of Muñoz's most effective and long-standing objective vehicles is the floor. In the early balconies and banisters the sculptural form emphasized a charged relationship with the preexisting gallery floor. For instance, in *London Balcony* the viewer was compelled to traverse the ground, visually if not bodily, in order to fully encounter the work. Muñoz first challenged the neutrality of the floor in *Minaret for Otto Kurtz* (1984). He positioned a towerlike structure, which was topped by a small balcony, in the corner of a space covered by an oriental carpet. The richly patterned and colored carpet created a spatial and gestural complement to the minaret. In addition to amplifying the sculpture's formal dimension, the carpet determined a metaphorical zone. In effect, the carpet allowed the esthetic concept to transcend the specificity of a gallery location and ultimately of a strictly formal interpretation.

The carpet rapidly evolved into room-size floor pieces. *The Waste Land* (1986), which has been remade in several versions, incorporates an illusionistically patterned floor that completely fills an enclosed room.[3] Opposite the entrance to the space is a strange bronze figure perched on a low, wall-mounted shelf. The figure, a ventriloquist's dummy in bronze, sits with legs dangling over the edge of the shelf. The floor and figure merge into a seamlessly integrated whole.

The use of an ornamental floor draws its inspiration from Islamic design, the first traces of which Muñoz exhibited in *Minaret for Otto Kurtz*. The artist intends not to replicate the precise visual principles developed during the flourishing of Islam in Spain from the eighth to fifteenth centuries. Rather, he seeks to engage the spirit of his influences, reflecting a discriminating and fragmented cultural memory. In fact, Islamic design concentrated more on rigorous geometric abstraction than on spatial illusion. Muñoz relies on optical patterning not for decorative value but as a means to create the illusion of a nonstatic or fluctuating space. One's movement across the floor of *The Waste Land* activates the sense that the ground itself is in motion. The apparent shift in surface distorts the viewer's notion of visual stability and triggers a sensation of restlessness.

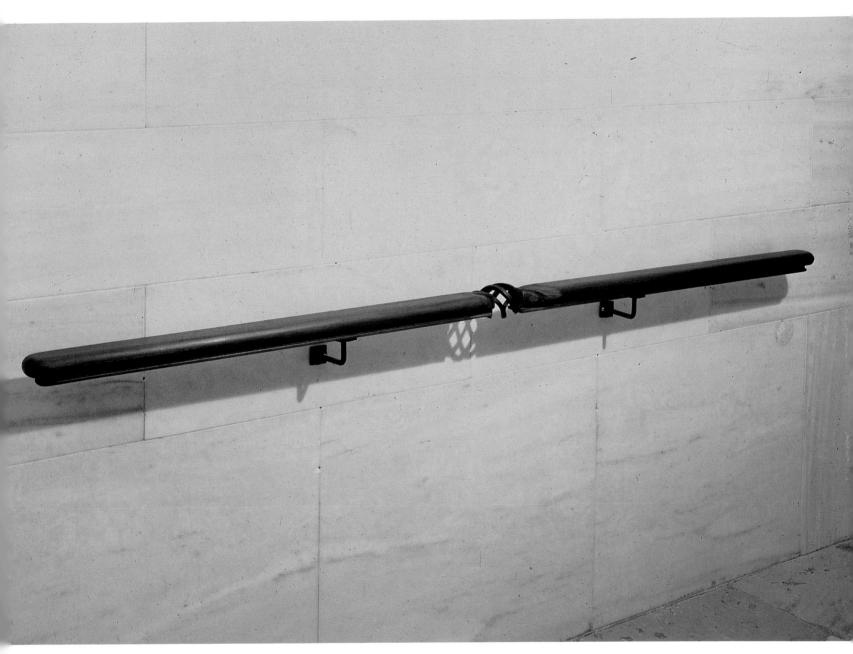

Favorite Banister, 1988
mixed media
3 1/4 x 86 x 3 1/4 in.
(8 x 220 x 8 cm)
Galería Marga Paz, Madrid

All in all, Muñoz's dummy is embroiled in a vision of strangeness. The grubby, mannered appearance of the patinated figure sharply contrasts with the geometric precision and finesse of the floor, creating a tense banter of incongruities. The floor-as-bridge leads from an engagingly beautiful foreground, desolate though it may be, to the embodiment of the grotesque. The dummy imitates the human physique, yet as a living entity it is utterly nonhuman. Muñoz himself has referred to it as an automaton.

In *The Identity of Departure* (1987) and *Study on the Diaphragm of The Ventriloquist* (1987), the dummy has been replaced by equally peculiar characters. The two more recent figures are assemblies of parts pieced together like robotic contraptions. Both are lifeless creatures that refer to the body of man only in mechanistic terms. These hollow forms, entrapped in environments of desolate beauty, relate in spirit to a tradition of twentieth-century Spanish literature and film referred to as *esperpento*. The term can best be translated as a grostesque or macabre tale. Manifested most thoroughly by the writings of Ramon del Valle-Inclan, *esperpento* presents a weird and almost unholy marriage of the beautiful and the grotesque.

After the ventriloquist's dummy had fulfilled its role, Muñoz enlisted the figure of a dwarf, which he continues to use. The dummies, dwarfs, and automatons are all aberrations of the human form. They appear as both innocent objects of pity and sinister projections. In *Three Columns* (1988) Muñoz grossly accentuates the overt physical imperfection and awkwardness of the dwarf by placing it in the context of three enormous, spiraling columns. In *Untitled* (1988) the gnome's stance atop a table raises him to a nearly normal height. Curiously, he holds a small, intricately inlaid wooden box that recalls the patterning of the artist's floors. Like the bronze ventriloquist's dummy, the dwarf personifies unreality. His clearly articulated unattractiveness, particularly in direct contrast to his surrounding environment, registers in the viewer feelings of discomfort and displacement. It is to this dominion of the unfamiliar and the intangible that the artist offers transit.

Lacquered Feet, 1989, wood, terra cotta, iron, Galería Marga Paz, Madrid

Muñoz's use of haunting forms dates back to the Galeria Vijande installation of 1984 that included *General Miaja Looking for the Guadiana River*. Gestural, half-body puppet figures were tightly packed in several of the tower structures. They more resembled archaeological fragments retrieved from a distant past than their human references. In recent works, such as *Lacquered Feet* (1989), body fragments are injected into incongruous surroundings. Muñoz rests a pair of detached wooden legs, feet pointing downward, over the edge of a shelf of an exquisitely constructed antique chest. He transforms human representations into inanimate artifacts. The unexpected combination of the elements, of the strange and the beautiful, results once again in a sensation tinged with anxiety and uneasiness.

*Study of The Ventriloquist's
Diaphragm*, 1987
mixed media
dimensions variable
Galería Marga Paz, Madrid

In *Floor with Balcony* (1987) Muñoz's contrived floor surface only partially fills the room. It is a rich, swirling wood grain pattern set within a geometric black frame and stretches out like a carpet in front of the rectangular, wrought-iron balcony. The effect is one of fluid, undulating motion. *A Metallic Object* (1988) proposes a far more agitated environment. A tightly ordered zig-zag pattern of black and white covers the expanse of the gallery floor. Viewed from the entrance of the space, the design reverberates nervously like an enormous Bridget Riley painting. A face mask, set within a capital-like architectural fragment, is mounted in the center of each of the space's three walls. The masks face downward, their gazes frozen on the restless floor. At first glance the room disguises itself as sparsely installed quarters in an archeological museum. However, the out-of-kilter characteristics of the objects and environment quickly and dramatically act to alter thoroughly one's reading of the space. Common to all of these spaces is the undeniable absence of activity. They appear to be devoid of life. *The Waste Land* envisions a realm of barren nothingness; yet implicit in Muñoz's setting is the suspicion of hidden meaning lurking beneath the veil of vacuity. Clearly deriving his title from that of the 1922 poem by T. S. Eliot, Muñoz similarly refers to the sterility and uneasiness of modern life. However, this condition of absence functions also to accentuate the visual illusionism of the floor, enabling it to stimulate mentally generated action. In this way, Muñoz's rooms relate to qualities characteristic of Baroque architecture and design. Muñoz, who is an ardent admirer of the work of seventeenth-century Italian architect Francesco Borromini, is attracted to the "lack of serenity" that a Baroque interior instills in the viewer.[4]

As was true of the early balconies and banisters, the seeming emptiness implores the viewer to walk through the space and to become an active ingredient in the scenario. Upon entering the space, one steps onto a stage empowered with the allusion of passage. As the viewer walks, the journey is set in motion. Transit is both physical and metaphorical. The floor extends to the spectator a bridge or link, but one without a predetermined point of destination. "The floor doesn't matter much. What matters is the walking across it. This constant apparent change. Something that has to do not so much with moving as with wanting to move or, perhaps, with the stillness of exterior appearances. It's an image about the temptation to re-invent."[5]

The suggestion of passage in the floor pieces, as well as the banisters and balconies, carries with it an implied geography of "otherness." The "other" is embodied in absence, in the emptiness of the balcony, for example. In *The Waste Land* the "other" inhabits the mute form of the ventriloquist's dummy. The dummy initially appeared in the artist's drawings several years earlier. After first constructing the figure, Muñoz allowed it to occupy his studio and home for some time before giving it a sculptural role. He used the puppetlike figure in several pieces, adapting and readdressing it, formally and contextually, before he felt it had been depleted of its power. In its final appearance Muñoz covered the dummy's head with a box.

The unequivocal silence of Muñoz's bronze figure positions it in the realm of "otherness." A ventriloquist's dummy, traditionally a wooden puppet with movable parts, is endowed with speech only through the intervention of its human counterpart. The puppet remains silent until acted upon by human hand and voice. In this case the doll has been rendered perpetually silent. Its very materiality—bronze—has petrified the figure in an eternally silent void. Indeed, even the dummy's unfixed gaze accentuates the spell of silence. He looks in the general direction of the viewer, that is, across the space of the room. Though the gaze more or less connects the distance between the viewer and the dummy, the look can never establish a specific goal. This vagueness and anti-explicitness deposits a residue of mysterious inconclusiveness.

The Identity of Departure, 1987
mixed media installation
162 1/2 x 162 1/2 ft
(50 x 50 m)
Galerie Roger Pailhas, Marseille

Recently Muñoz has introduced a new series of figures. *Hunters* (1988) and *Untitled (Bending)* (1989) both incorporate generic male figures executed as flattened iron cutouts. Like shadow puppets, the hinged figures are anchored to mechanical arms that are in turn attached to wooden platforms. Lined up as if targets in a shooting gallery, the hunters are equipped with appropriate weapons and gear to carry out a hunt. Yet there is no action; the bending figures appear flexible but do not move. Both groups are locked in endless circles of frustration as they are denied their implicit function. Their nonactivity functions instead to register a process of questioning.

Throughout his work Muñoz has devised quizzical and often disturbing arrangements of objective clues as a means to stimulate mental exploration. His sculptures, both isolated figures and contextualized room installations, stand as vehicles through which the artist and viewer alike can pursue a goal of search rather than location. They mark and facilitate passage to territories determined and understood only by the imagination. Not unlike archaeological artifacts Muñoz has admired over the years, his sculptures give physical form to citizens of fantasy and myth.

Muñoz's pair of dragons in *Dragon Back* (1990)[6] are creatures that never have nor ever will partake in our quotidian existence. Yet they perform successfully as palpable manifestations of the imagination. Each bronze beast is stationed atop a pedestal marking the entrance to a space that they cohabit only with an illusionistic floor. Muñoz's creatures belong to a morphological category that is both organic and inorganic. The backs of the reptilian bodies are covered with a diamond pattern that delights the eye as it distinguishes between what is animal and what is design. In this case Muñoz's geometric design derives from Giotto's fourteenth-century frescoes in the Arena Chapel in central Italy. Giotto employed the pattern as a decorative device that endowed his two-dimensional biblical scenes with a more physical, architectural context.

The dragons, like the dwarfs and the ventriloquist's dummy, herald the possibility of "otherness." Their emphasis on irreality, nonactivity, and vacancy actually operates to facilitate passage to a temporality of a different order. They give shape and tangible substance to the illogic and unchartability of internal musings. "I build metaphors in the guise of sculpture, because I do not know any other way to explain to myself what it is that troubles me."[7]

Lucinda Barnes

NOTES

1. Conversation with the artist, November 1989.
2. Muñoz no longer incorporates the banister, balcony, or ventriloquist's dummy in his work.
3. *The Waste Land* has been executed and reproduced in separate variations. The main difference has been in the execution of the floor. Though the illusionistic principle remained the same, Muñoz altered color schemes as well as materials.
4. *Juan Muñoz* (Bordeaux: capc Museé d'art contemporain, 1984), p. 44.
5. Ibid.
6. This work has been created specifically for the Newport Harbor Art Museum. Although closely related to *Two Painted Dragons* and *Dwarf with Parallel Lines* (1989), installed at Lisson Gallery, London, in September 1989, *Dragon Back* concentrates on a more optically patterned floor and does not include the figure of the dwarf.
7. *Juan Muñoz*, p. 44.

A Metallic Object, 1988
mixed media
dimensions variable
Galería Marga Paz, Madrid

The Waste Land at Fontevraud,
1987
Installation at Abbaye Royal,
Fontevraud, France
paint on plastic ground, bronze
47 in. x 26 ft. 6 in.
(120 x 820 cm)
Galería Marga Paz, Madrid

The Waste Land, 1986
mixed media
dimensions variable
Galería Marga Paz, Madrid

Untitled, 1988
terra cotta, wood
33 1/4 x 15 3/4 in.
(85 x 40 cm)
Galería Marga Paz, Madrid

Three Columns, 1988
terra cotta
dimensions variable
Galería Marga Paz, Madrid

The Hunters, 1988
wood, iron
76 1/2 x 80 3/4 x 19 1/2 in.
(196 x 207 x 50 cm)
Galería Marga Paz, Madrid

Untitled (Bending), 1989
wood, iron
72 x 8 x 20 1/4 in.
(184 x 20 x 52 cm)
Galería Marga Paz, Madrid

Opposite:
Two Painted Dragons and *Dwarf
with Parallel Lines*, 1989
Installation at Lisson Gallery,
London
mixed media
dimensions variable
Lisson Gallery, London

Left:
Detail from
Two Painted Dragons, 1989
bronze
Lisson Gallery, London

JULIAN OPIE

A criticism voiced often about Julian Opie's painted steel sculptures of the early 1980s was that their reverse sides are inert. To make those works, Opie typically cut the profiles of an image from sheet steel, bent, creased and welded them into puffy volumetric shapes, and painted their exterior surfaces to give them figural identities. His recent work is crafted all round and occupies social and psychological space (and time) very differently.

Images of things such as credit cards, parking tickets, tools, packs of candy or cigarettes, kitchenware, and sometimes numerals and words spelled out in folded letters, comprise the early sculptures. Some pieces involve brusque repaintings of famous pictures or generic reprises of abstract sculpture with nonsignifying shapes painted to become cartoonish images of themselves.

Whether they hang on a wall, rest on the floor or on a tabletop, these sculptures almost always have a "dead" side: the unpainted, artless obverse of the jaunty face they turn to the world. Typically there is nothing to prevent viewers from inspecting the unadorned facets of such a piece. Opie believes (and I agree) that the strength of these sculptures is in the dreamy looseness of their illusionism and its unresolved relation to bald structural facts their back views betray. These works reiterate the point that becoming absorbed in an image—even in sculpture—involves disattending to how it is made. For this reason, sculpture can heighten and sustain the tension between obliviousness and conscious observation. Opie found he could give this psychological tension physical reverberations that would echo outward into the realm of objects that we inhabit with no thought of art, often with no thought at all. In this manner sculpture becomes a

means to question the arrangements and transactions we call the world. Opie accomplished this in his early work by overt uses of representation. In more recent work, his sculpture's objective character—its resitance to easy recognition—transmits its skeptical force. Front and back views of the *Night Lights* are in the same psychological key: there is no shift here (as there is in the early work) between material and rhetorical facts. All the *Night Lights'* aspects contribute to their paradoxical force of being things whose forms are carefully calculated and whose significance is indeterminate and seemingly marginal to familiar realities.

In his early pieces, Opie showed that not everything about how representation works can be clarified using images. His recent work eliminates images without banishing reference or being abstract. Where his early work tapped domestic or studio life—stuff that was in his pockets, his hands, or his head, all of it having public reality—the recent sculptures relate overtly to the furniture of public places such as airports, supermarkets, and office buildings. The new work's quotient of representation is harder to estimate: it relates uncertainly to things such as vending machines and portable backlit billboards. We cannot tell when faced with the *Night Lights* whether their functions are apparent or hidden, commercial or ritual, public or psychic.

G, 1987
glass, aluminum, stainless
steel, foam, PVC, wood,
cellulose paint
25 x 70 3/4 x 33 1/2 in.
(63.5 x 181 x 86 cm)
Saatchi Collection, London

The recognition that imagery is a special case of representation lies behind all of Opie's work. Representation in the large sense encompasses our use of things as symbols to negotiate relations, both with each other and between aspects of ourselves, that we see as disjunctive or as inscrutably linked. The industries of advertising, entertainment and social propaganda supply countless opportunities for psychic (and consumer) investment in products and spectacles that purport to alter our sense of ourselves and our fancied advantages in life. A perfume or shaving lotion purports to change our feelings about ourselves and enables us to behave more confidently or seductively. Cars are marketed as devices that will bring new freedom and social pride to their overworked owners. The emotional transactions crisscrossing the conduct of human relationships through commodities are rarely articulated. Their occasional ironic acknowledgment in advertising serves only to solidify the belief that they need not be spoken about because they are already part of common psychic parlance. Most of the intimate uses of representation that spin off the civic landmarks of billboards, of magazine and television ads remain unconscious. Everyday—and necessary—consumer choices are burdened with a weight of specious, fantasied importance that, taken to heart, intensifies the moral and practical difficulty of living. This is the social condition to which all of Opie's art responds.

In his early work, Opie showed how the psychic burden of representations in media-driven culture could be borne lightly. He made like an acrobat, figuratively balancing a stack of masterpieces here, there a clutch of gargantuan tools or an "abstract" sculpture. No problem if they all clatter to the floor: more can always be made. Neither authenticity nor irreplaceability is an issue. For Opie these sculptures were also an opportunity to juggle canonical principles of modernism, such as truth to materials and the incommensurability of abstraction and imagery.

Opie's early sculptures are not just images. They are composed of images and of what images are com-

Lonely Abroad, 1985, oil paint on steel, 56 x 36 x 36 in. (137.1 x 91.4 91.4 cm)   Private collection, London

posed of: materials, decisions, recognizable references, illustrative conventions and, on the spectator's part, ingrained responses. The way Opie painted these sculptures—with a brisk, easy, summary touch—displays, as its effects, pictorial suggestion. Similarly, as husks of metal, the sculptures are assembled and fastened with casual articulation. The work is put together so that we can see how all its aspects function, like gourmets who savor a dish while discerning the role of each ingredient. You might say these sculptures are devices for magnifying some of the pleasures of art, as suggested by their caricatural humor and their imagistic enlargements of things. Cocky and close to home, they made post-pop vaudeville of the gaps that separate representations, what they represent, and what they are made of. These gaps rattle with questions: how do we come to accept one construction as the representation of another? Why is not the specificity of things always more vivid to us than their representational "exchange value" or than the fantasies we project upon them? Is life in corporate consumer society primarily a play of representations that people carry on unconsciously by means of things? What would happen to this process were we to become sportively conscious of it?

A., 1987
aluminum, stainless steel,
foam, PVC, wood, cellulose
paint
7 3/4 x 37 3/4 x 144 3/4 in.
each
(19.7 x 95.8 x 367.7 cm)
Lisson Gallery, London

The new work seen in this exhibition is hermetic and sinister by comparison to what preceded it. Its hallmark is precisely that we cannot tell how its elements function or what their functioning means. (In some respects, these works are carefully fitted out to satisfy our casual sense of something electrical that runs.) In 1987 Opie began making objects that look something like food shop display cases or possibly laboratory appliances: glass-paneled cabinets (upright, floor-bound, or affixed to the wall). Another series resembles air conditioning vents. The freestanding, fridge-like objects are clad in glossy white vinyl on all but one side. Through their glass fronts, you can see silvery metallic interior walls. Shelves of glass articulate the insides of some pieces. Opie works hard to give these handmade objects the look of industrially fabricated products. He does this not just for irony's sake but as a challenge to our ability to sense the kind of effort and intent an object embodies. There is a calculated absurdity to Opie's labor of handcrafting things to look factory-made. It is like an impersonation of alienated labor and is part of his project to make "something that's completely ignorable that, once you notice it, seems extraordinary." Humor is involved here, as in his earlier work, but it is carefully submerged.

The esthetics of Opie's sculpture from the past three years bring to mind the gleaming open boxes of Donald Judd—some metal, some metal-lined or topped with plexiglass—which are industrially fabricated. The ventlike structures Opie has made to hang on or hug to the wall recall the repetitive structures made by Judd and Robert Morris in the mid-1960s. But where Judd and Morris did everything possible to avoid reference, Opie toys with his objects' affinities both to their sculpture and to functional hardware and its settings.

Julian Opie's studio, London, 1988

In its look of dubious purpose, Opie's recent work relates to the "commodity" sculpture of Haim Steinbach and Jeff Koons, especially to Koons's fluorescent-lit vacuum cleaners and basketball-bobbing aquariums. But there is always a hint of fellow-feeling for the viewer in Opie's art that is not felt in the works of Koons and Steinbach. Opie's "appliance" works are neither prefabricated objects nor smart-aleck simulacra. Their mark is to be at home neither in the no-man's-land of workaday civic life nor in the safe haven of museum and gallery, yet to vibrate with echoes of both.

The works in the *Night Lights* series vibrate literally, too, with the low hum of fans installed in them solely to enhance the objects' affinity to vending machines, refrigerated display cases, or whatever they happen to recall to those who see them. All of them resemble giant light boxes of the sort used to view slides or x-ray transparencies. The sense that they are devices for viewing something else jostles with one's assumption that they are artistic ends in themselves.

Stripped of interior detail and fitted with concealed fluorescents that give them foggy halations of interior light, these objects are larger than those that preceded them, slightly larger than you. The softly pulsating bands of light at their front margins relate to the brushy lines that give representational contours to the painted shapes in Opie's early sculpture. Both visual devices solicit imaginative resolution—closure by reading—on our part, but in the new work we are given no clue how to accomplish this.

J, 1987
glass, aluminum, stainless
steel, foam, PVC, wood
49 3/4 x 84 3/4 x 10 3/4 in.
(127 x 217 x 27 cm)
Saatchi Collection, London

The reverse sides of the new works incorporate details—vents, grates, switches, and cord hooks—that have no real meaning or function except to fulfill our expectation that an object that appears to have internal workings must include gear for operating them. The cords that run from these sculptures to the wall were originally needed only to power the works' light fixtures; the fans were an afterthought. Yet part of what makes the objects seem familiar at first, or acceptable, is our own ignorance of their workings: most of us are comfortable not knowing how mundane gadgets and systems—from light switches to governments' tactics of social control—work. In his recent sculpture Opie calls attention to our acceptance of and dependence on a world of things whose workings we could come to understand but likely do not. His sculptures look unremarkable at first because they appear to fall into the category of things whose function is familiar but whose operation is mysterious to us. Opie intensifies the strangeness of his *Night Lights* by making them look a bit old-fashioned, like very forward-looking devices from the late 1950s, say, whose large dimensions are due to their predating more recent advances in miniaturization. So they set us to wondering whether their function is obscure to us because we're too young or due to gaps in our memory. (Also they must make different impressions depending on whether you encounter them in America, Europe, or the Third World.)

When you are conscious of representation as an issue in contemporary culture, you see that there may be more at issue here than the disquieting effect of a familiar-looking artifact turning out to be unknown and cryptic. The play of engagement and obliviousness that marked Opie's early sculpture marks the recent work in a very different way. Instead of a tension between beguiling imagery and its unglamorized support, the new work confronts us with our preference for ignorance when faced with banal realities whose implications and interconnectedness are more than we care to think about. Perhaps our acceptance of mystification is merely practical, the demands of life allowing us so little time to understand life's devices. Then again, as Martin Heidegger believed, technology may just define a mode of human reality that is profoundly self-alienating, being the symptom of an unconscious collective project of evading the strangeness of existence.

Opie's sculpture lends itself to interpretation on these lines. The central experience it offers is one of intensifying estrangement from objects that at first appear almost ordinary and redundant. Like the fluorescent light works of Dan Flavin, which are part of their ancestry, Opie's appliance-like objects slowly turn our attention from the space to the time they occupy. One way to understand them is as devices for clarifying the quality of "ambient time," of late twentieth-century time in the First World. In the experience of time they impose, we recognize the sensations of waiting for things to come clearer in a world that increasingly presents itself both as man-made and as out of control, as more unintelligible the more it is subjected to human projects. Opie's *Night Lights* function as mirrors, not of appearances but of the lived quality of time. (Several even resemble high-tech wardrobes faced with full-length mirrors; this aspect of them brings Roy Lichtenstein and Richard Artschwager to mind.) The *Night Lights* confront you with time as one more metered product of industry, connected to the power company and other corporate deities, but a different element altogether from the immemorial cycles of daylight, darkness, and seasons.

Kenneth Baker

n.o., 1988
plastic, glass, aluminum, wood,
rubber, cellulose paint
67 1/4 x 24 1/4 x 25 3/4 in.
each
(172 x 62 x 66 cm)
Lisson Gallery, London

Night Light 16/2222CC, 1989
rubber, aluminum, glass,
plastic, wood, stainless steel,
fluorescent light, cellulose paint
72 3/4 x 48 1/2 x 15 3/4 in.
(186 x 124 x 40 cm)
Courtesy Lisson Gallery,
London

Opposite: front view
Left: back view

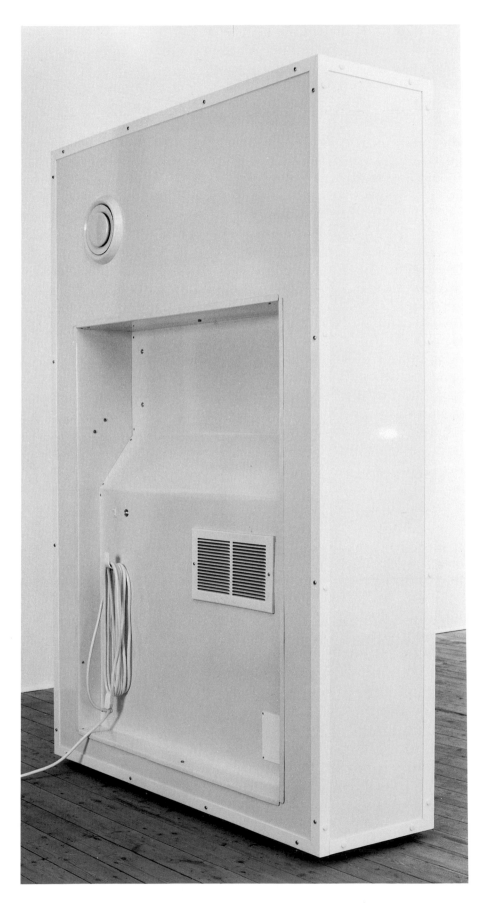

Night Light 25/3333CB, 1989
wood, glass, rubber, aluminum,
cellulose paint, fluorescent
light, plastic
72 3/4 x 48 1/2 x 16 1/2 in.
(186 x 124 x 42 cm)
Courtesy Lisson Gallery,
London

Opposite: front view
Left: back view

Night Light 19/1343GY, 1989
rubber, aluminum, glass,
plastic, wood, stainless steel,
fluorescent light, cellulose paint
73 x 48 x 17 3/4 in.
(187 x 123 x 45 cm)
Courtesy Lisson Gallery,
London

Opposite: front view
Left: back view

Night Light 21/2222BB, 1989
rubber, aluminum, glass,
plastic, wood, stainless steel,
fluorescent light
73 1/2 x 48 x 15 3/4 in.
(188 x 123 x 40 cm)
Courtesy Lisson Gallery,
London

Opposite: front view
Left: back view

Night Light 26/5444CY, 1989
wood, glass, rubber, anodized
aluminum, zincoid, fluorescent
light
72 3/4 x 48 1/2 x 15 3/4 in.
(186 x 124 x 40 cm)
Courtesy Lisson Gallery,
London

Opposite: front view
Left: back view

HAIM STEINBACH

Detail from *Untitled (elephant foot stools, elephant skull)*, 1988

In the catalog for the 1988 exhibition *The Binational*, Haim Steinbach says, "I use Minimalism and Structuralism as thinking philosophies."[1] It is necessary here to understand the term "structuralist" in a sense that is authentic and far-removed from any epigonic theoretical usage. The word defines, in effect, beyond the exactness and strictness of the artistic process (this would be the "Duchamp side" of Haim Steinbach), its own dimension within language. To be more precise, a great line of demarcation divides art today into two main halves: let's call them, in global terms, the formalist world and the conceptualist method. Without ever really separating the two, this demarcation is present, in a subtle and discreet manner, at the core of Steinbach's work.

The artist himself is quite conscious of the genesis of his work, which he precisely conceives as an interrogation of the way in which the use of objects already functions *as a language*:

> I am interested in the way people make choices in collecting things and what it involves. Collectively, social customs of appreciating objects by using them, arranging and placing them in various ways in different contexts function *as a language.*[2]

What matters here is not the identity with language, but the "as if." This false analogy will constitute the basis of "language" itself in Steinbach's art (I am using the word "language" here in a very general sense) so that it is necessary in strict terms—I'm thinking here of Roman Jakobson—to describe the two fundamental operations of language: selection and arrangement. One of these is at once preferential—selection. This asymmetry of function sets in motion all the forces of humor and irony. Jorge Luis Borges knew this, so that the "Library of Babel" is based on the inverse operation: *as if* language were based *only* upon arrangement. As for arrangement, Steinbach pulls it out of a universe of signs (which would suffice to distinguish him from all the artists in the tow of semiotics), while making it spill into the material:

> One may say that an object speaks in a different way, or tells a different story, *depending on its grouping with other objects.*[3]

In terms of structural exactness, then, we must say, on one hand, that a sort of anamorphosis of language is created by a reduction of original function, and, on the other hand, that the method of exhibiting objects comes to speak for what is an impossible language. If this presentation were metaphorical, if, by its selective way of grouping objects, it had significance as a cultural token (if it were thus more ironic than humorous, more critical than affirmative —as is evident in the work of a number of young New York artists today), this style of exhibiting would compensate for any loss of meaning; by some ironic pirouette, in the final instance, artistic intervention would summon forth the supremacy of its decision. Now, what precisely characterizes the work of Haim Steinbach is that this refusal of

sweetest taboo, 1987
mixed media construction
20 1/8 x 72 x 14 in.
(51.1 x 182.8 x 35.5 cm)
Collection Staatsgalerie Stuttgart,
Courtesy Lia Rumma, Naples

Detail from *Untitled (elephant foot stools, elephant skull)*, 1988

critical mastery is the corollary of the first operation: certainly the selected objects form an arrangement, but this arrangement is determinedly paratactic, not syntactic. There is *mise-en-scène*, but here also the presentation stands against the concept. Once again, the language is perverted and subverted by the exclusive use of metonymy. The stories these objects tell and the difference in their languages depend upon the absolute way in which they are grouped. The dependence is not of subordination, but of coordination: it is exactly because the conjunction stands ("this" . . . "this" . . . and "this") that the objects become subjects. The director delegates all their powers to them. They distance themselves from all strategic value (they are no longer pawns on the chessboard of the concept of art); they start to become, as it were, characters.[4]

Needless to say, despite appearances, we are now at opposition with Duchamp's position. The readymade is, by its very nature, alone. This is not by chance, since the uniqueness of the object refers to the series from which it was taken and in which it is no

longer a component. To the degree that the object is used in an industrial sense, it functions as a war machine aimed at the aura of the artwork; as a unique piece, it maintains, in a dialectical sense, absolute artistic authority. It seems that this paradox could not be taken much further. Steinbach's work demonstrates that this dialectic can and must be broken down. Just as he arranges objects *as if* they were a language and gives them their role and their voice, by divesting them of their semiotic function, he gives back to the objects their plurality, their silent community, against the supreme act of auto-affirmation of concept ("that's art"). This is a subtle reversal, since, as demonstrated, by abandoning the sentence he nevertheless maintains art. It is the same paradox of minimal function and even more forceful than the difference between art and non-art,[5] but the sophisticated Duchampian machinery is turned against itself.

At first, it's as if a *division of power* takes place. The readymade was only the *material support* of the concept in its manner of intervention. Steinbach contests this domain, this centrality of concept and pleads in favor of the multiplicity of objects. An object is an object,[6] but, above all, an object is never alone. There are no single objects, there are only environments, multiplicities, and when the object appears, it is only something that detaches itself from a context of whose language it speaks:

> The choice of *an* object in itself is not primary since any object derives its meaning through a set of relations between people and objects and the manner by which objects are made ready to relate with other objects (thus an object is a "made-ready-to-relate" rather than a "readymade").[7]

In the case of the readymade, the ironic subtraction that the object had to endure concerning its original function condemns it to remain forever the substratum of the sentences presenting the mode of its artistic intervention. Steinbach constructs a silent theater around his objects (and with them adds to the questions posed by the readymade), spaces of possibility in which the reconstructed form oscillates interminably between its synthetic nature (compositional) and its analytical nature (relational). The readymade sufficed unto itself; it was set upon the

Untitled (doll carriage, cameras),
1988
mixed media construction
26 3/4 x 88 x 18 1/2 in.
(68 x 223.5 x 47 cm)
Collection Centre Georges
Pompidou, Courtesy Jay
Gorney Modern Art, New York,
and Sonnabend Gallery,
New York

Detail from *Untitled (elephant foot stools, elephant skull)*, 1988

immutable and intangible pedestal of its constitutive negation: "this is not (any longer) a urinal, a bottle-rack, a snow shovel, etc." In Haim Steinbach's work, the object has the right to keep its original qualities (memory retained and blotted out by its use, by its preference, by all its formal, material and institutional qualities, infinitely variable), while, from now on, ceasing to exhaust itself in their definition.

After 1984, the base materializes in a formal positiveness exactly contrary to that of Duchamp. In place of the underlying negation, the conceptual affirmation ("this is art") takes form: exact, severe, cold and beautiful as an industrial object, indifferent and obsessed at the same time. The base performs the passage from the formula "this is no longer an object, but what is art?" to the formula "this is (really) art, but what can be an object?" So here we stop overworking, ad infinitum, the initial

disruption of the negation: this is *still* a box of corn-flakes, a portable radio, an elephant skull, a stuffed bear, etc. In the readymade the number of questions asked was limited; here the multiplicity of objects (from unusual, droll, (post)modern bric-a-brac that surrounds us to the most exacting selections of the collector) becomes the focus of work and interrogation.

The continuity of this project is as remarkable as the process of its refinement. Since 1979, Steinbach has shifted more and more from the question of contextuality (the dialectic of place and function, the museum/institution and its subversion of art, and, in general, the game of interior-exterior) to the exactness of presentation.

From the 1979 exhibitions at Artists Space and the Johnson Museum to the present, the artistic ground covered is immense. In work created before 1984, the "language" that the objects "speak" is still chatty; its grammar is explicit and the artistic process is revealed in a wider sense. For example, at the Johnson Museum, a Herbert Ferber sculpture was coexhibited with a shelf displaying the facsimile of a pre-Columbian object and a plastic ball, and a red shirt was fastened to a wall covered with several indescribably gaudy sections of wallpaper. The composition of this installation sets forth, in an explicit manner, the conflicting relation between the method of artistic intervention and its contexts. This was a matter of preparing and dealing with things in the questioning of structures. The conflict between the exhibitive and the nonexhibitive was revealed and, on the material plane, was deployed from one object to another, from their cohabitation to their *mise-en-scène*, from their *mise-en-scène* to their place of *mise-en-scène*, etc.

The questioning of criteria and the articulation of the installation tended to multiply the number of structures interrogated, all the while minimalizing the process of their presentation.[8] We only have to consider the works since 1984-85 to realize what has happened. If it is true that each work of art, independent of the concept of art itself, can be considered as art by its capacity of breaking down in a sort of unending collapsing of its own difference, and if it is true that this power transcends every artistic code and every "callistique,"[9] we must then

common standard, 1987
mixed media construction
40 1/2 x 54 x 17 1/2 in.
(102.9 x 137.2 x 44.5 cm)
Collection Camille and Paul
Oliver-Hoffmann, Courtesy
Rhona Hoffmann Gallery,
Chicago

Detail from *Untitled (elephant foot stools, elephant skull)*, 1988

say of this second period of Steinbach's work that it represents henceforth an asymptotic approach to the same question. In a moment of continuous reduction, the tensions between object and artifact, between chance selection and the exactness of *mise-en-scène*, are, on one hand, exacerbated and, on the other, blended more and more with the internal relation of the arrangement.[10]

The objects, rescued from the din of artistic codes, uses, and requirements, enter silently into a tense anticipation of an archaeological future to which they belong in advance. An "artful balance" between contrasts (memory-amnesia, unusual-banal, death-sleep, art object-kitchen utensil, black-white, or whatever) maintains, in subtle oscillation, appearance and meaning, the indifference of the utensil and the commanding presence of an increasingly demanding formal articulation. The game of differences and identities is regulated with clockwork precision. The yes and no echo in a play upon a surface where shadow is forbidden.

The choice of materials (woods, lacquers, as well as the substance of the objects) is essential. Thanks to this, the objects acquire an astonishing seductive power. The narcissistic reflection of the objects—neither mirror nor opaqueness—forbids simultaneous indifference and interpretation; these "made-ready-to-relates" will never cross the threshold of words. Words echo; dreams are snatched from the commercial void; all are kept in a subliminal presence just before or just after the meaning. Their retention responds to the silent dialogue of objects, waiting for a meaning—perhaps: "Rêvez, nous"[11]

Jean-Pierre Dubost
(Translation: Gabrielle Daughtry)

NOTES

1. *The Binational, American Art of the Late '80s.* (Boston: The Institute of Contemporary Art and Museum of Fine Arts; Cologne: Dumont Buchverlag, 1989), p. 192.
2. Quote from a letter from Haim Steinbach, unpublished.
3. Ibid. (Author's emphasis.)
4. "Lining them up on a shelf-ledge. . .Steinbach creates a horizon-line of 'figures' that range from the elegant to the vulgar, from cold to sensual, from elitist to kitsch, from mobile to static, and from opaque to lustrous. They have all been wrenched from a gray existence to be 'revealed' or 'staged', thereby conquering darkness and fear, and becoming intriguing silhouettes or actors." Germano Celant, in *Haim Steinbach.* (Bordeaux: capc Musée d'art contemporain, 1988), p. 15.

Untitled (sandals, chair), 1987
mixed media construction
25 1/2 x 57 1/8 x 21 1/4 in.
(64.8 x 145.1 x 54 cm)
Collection Silvio Sansone,
Courtesy Lia Rumma, Naples

Detail from *Untitled (elephant foot stools, elephant skull)*, 1988

5. "There is an antique store in New York City, on Second Avenue, which I often pass by. One day I noticed a group of objects arranged by the proprietor in the window. Two small 17th-century figures carved in wood, a friar and a nun, stood side by side. A few inches away stood a pair of 18th-century iron locks from Spain. Rather than lying on their sides, as would normally be expected, these locks were upright with their iron rods (for the latch) aiming at an angle upwards. After passing by this window on several occasions, I realized that the arrangement was definitive in its own right, so I bought the objects." Haim Steinbach, unpublished letter. This is like Duchamp's encounter with the chocolate grinder in the shop window in Rouen, but perhaps it's even more like Apollinaire's strolls in "The Stroller of Two River Banks" as he discovers quite by chance the compelling presence of unusual objects.

6. "For me, a thing is not a device for universal statements, and, therefore, an object is an object, not a readymade." Haim Steinbach, "Notes on Duchamp and the Aesthetic Emotion," unpublished.

7. Ibid.

8. The installation at Artists Space further extended the contextual game into the auditive by integrating into the installation a tape recorder playing a selection of fragments of popular songs.

9. From a 1913 note in the writings of Marcel Duchamp: "Le possible est seulement un 'mordant' physique brûlant toute esthétique ou callistique." (The possible is only an all-consuming physical burning up the esthetic or callistic.) *Écrits* (Paris: Flammarion, 1975), p. 104.

10. From 1980 to 1984 one can say that Haim Steinbach's work hovers between the principle of contextual extension and the principle of ulterior condensation. It was in 1980 that the idea of presenting objects on the pedestal support appeared, while at the same time the anarchic showing of objects was accentuated in the extreme. This was the same case for the installation at Fashion Moda in the South Bronx and the same for the installation at Bell Art Gallery (Brown University), 1982. The "Shelf Arrangements," installed in apartments between 1980 and 1981, can be considered as the explicit cohabitation of two principles. In 1981 and 1982 the socle (pedestal) clearly affirmed itself, but the use of wallpaper upheld the principle of contextual allusion. But after 1984 everything changed: whether it was *mise-en-scène* on the socle or "in the box" (as in *Untitled (daybed, coffin)*), what matters is the materialization of the support entering into dialogue with the objects. The differentiation of supports and the frameworks is the corollary of the condensation of objects.

11. "Rêvez, nous"—which literally means "(you) dream, we"—is a sentence fragment taken out of context from a French travel agency's advertising slogan, which reads "Rêvez, nous feront le reste." (Dream, we will do the rest.) This fragment was blown up and painted on a wall at the Bordeaux exhibition of Steinbach's work in 1988.

*Untitled (elephant foot stools,
elephant skull)*, 1988
mixed media construction
Foot stool shelf:
44 x 128 x 23 1/4 in.
(111.7 x 325.1 x 59 cm)
Skull shelf:
88 1/2 x 43 x 41 1/2 in.
(224.7 x 109.2 x 105.4 cm)
Collection of the artist, Courtesy
Jay Gorney Modern Art, New
York, and Sonnabend Gallery,
New York

Opposite:
Adirondack tableau, 1988
mixed media installation
108 x 264 x 66 1/2 in.
(274.3 x 670.6 x 169 cm)
Sonnabend Gallery, New York,
and Jay Gorney Modern Art,
New York

Left:
Detail from
Adirondack tableau

Untitled (French walnut armoire,
Cuban mahogany armoire),
1988
Installation at capc Musée
d'art contemporain, Bordeaux
mixed media construction
122 1/4 x 107 3/4 x 79 in.
(310.5 x 273.7 x 200.7 cm)
Collection Lia Rumma, Courtesy
Sonnabend Gallery, New York,
and Jay Gorney Modern Art,
New York

Opposite: front view
Left: back view

Untitled (daybed, coffin), 1989
mixed media construction
69 3/8 x 101 1/2 x 82 1/8 in.
(175.8 x 257.8 x 208.6 cm)
Courtesy Sonnabend Gallery,
New York, and Jay Gorney
Modern Art, New York

Opposite: front view
Left: back view

CATALOG
OF THE
EXHIBITION

EXHIBITION
HISTORIES

SELECTED
BIBLIOGRAPHY

CATALOG OF THE EXHIBITION

Dimensions are given with height preceding width, width preceding depth.

GRENVILLE DAVEY

Untitled, 1990
painted steel
two parts: 62 3/4 x 17 1/2 in.
each
(161 x 45 cm)
Courtesy Lisson Gallery, London

Untitled, 1990
painted MDF (composite board),
steel
76 x 7 3/4 in.
(191 x 20 cm)
Courtesy Lisson Gallery, London

Untitled, 1990
painted steel
76 x 7 3/4 in.
(191 x 20 cm)
Courtesy Lisson Gallery, London

KATHARINA FRITSCH

Ghost and Pool of Blood, 1988
polyester resin, plexiglas
Ghost: 78 3/4 x 23 1/2 in.
(200 x 59.7 cm)
Blood: 21 x 82 1/2 in.
(53.5 x 209.6 cm)
Collection Ydessa Hendeles,
Courtesy Ydessa Hendeles Art
Foundation

ROBERT GOBER

Playpen, 1987
wood and enamel paint
26 1/8 x 39 x 39 in.
(66.3 x 99.1 x 99.1 cm)
Saatchi Collection, London

Plywood, 1987
laminated fir
95 x 46 1/2 x 5/8 in.
(242 x 118.1 x 1.6 cm)
Collection Andrew Ong, Courtesy
Paula Cooper Gallery

Untitled (door and doorframe),
1987-88
mixed media
Door: 84 x 34 x 1 1/2 in.
(213.4 x 86.4 x 3.8 cm)
Doorframe: 90 x 43 x 5 1/2 in.
(228.6 x 109.2 x 14 cm)
Private collection

Hanging Man/Sleeping Man
wallpaper, 1989
silkscreen on paper
Courtesy Paula Cooper Gallery,
New York

Untitled Leg, 1989-90
wax, cotton, wood, leather,
human hair
12 1/2 x 5 x 20 in.
Courtesy Paula Cooper Gallery,
New York

JEFF KOONS

Louis (XIV), 1986
stainless steel
46 x 27 x 15 in.
(116.8 x 68.5 x 38.1 cm)
Collection of the artist, Courtesy
Sonnabend Gallery

Italian Woman, 1986
stainless steel
30 x 18 x 11 in.
(76.2 x 45.7 x 27.9 cm)
Collection Leo Castelli

French Coach Couple, 1986
stainless steel
17 x 15 1/2 x 11 3/4 in.
(43.2 x 39.4 x 29.9 cm)
Private collection, Courtesy
Sonnabend Gallery

Flowers, 1986
stainless steel
12 1/2 x 18 x 12 in.
(31.8 x 45.7 x 30.5 cm)
Collection Barbara and
Richard S. Lane

Two Kids, 1986
stainless steel
23 x 14 1/2 x 14 1/4 in.
(58.4 x 36.2 x 36.2 cm)
Collection Mera and Donald
Rubell

Doctor's Delight, 1986
stainless steel
11 x 6 3/4 x 5 3/4 in.
(27.9 x 17.2 x 14.6 cm)
Courtesy Sonnabend Gallery,
New York

Cape Codder Troll, 1986
stainless steel
21 x 8 1/2 x 9 in.
(53.4 x 21.6 x 22.9 cm)
Collection Robert and
Honey Dootson

Mermaid Troll, 1986
stainless steel
20 1/2 x 8 1/2 x 8 1/2 in.
(52.1 x 21.6 x 21.6 cm)
Collection of the artist, Courtesy
Sonnabend Gallery

Bob Hope, 1986
stainless steel
17 x 5 1/2 x 5 1/2 in.
(43.2 x 14 x 14 cm)
Sonnabend Collection

Rabbit, 1986
stainless steel
41 x 19 x 12 in.
(104.1 x 48.2 x 30.5 cm)
Private collection

ANNETTE LEMIEUX
The Seat of the Intellect, 1984
oil on helmet
11 x 9 7/16 x 6 1/2 in.
(28 x 24 x 16.5 cm)
Collection of the artist, Courtesy
Josh Baer Gallery

Oh, Promise Me, 1985
typewriter, table, player piano
scroll
Scroll: 16 ft (5 meters)
Private collection, Switzerland

Sonnet, 1987
wood shelf, books, wood frame
50 x 33 x 5 1/2 in.
(127 x 83.8 x 13.9 cm)
Collection the artist, Courtesy
Josh Baer Gallery

Formal Wear, 1987
bronze, edition 9
9 3/4 x 69 1/4 x 23 1/4 in.
(24.8 x 175.9 x 59.1 cm)
Collection Eli and
Edythe L. Broad

Tall Tale, 1987
78 books, wood bookcase, text
66 x 10 1/2 x 8 1/4 in.
(167.6 x 26.7 x 21 cm)
Private collection,
Los Angeles

Two Short Stories, 1987
books, text
Left: 18 x 9 3/4 x 6 1/2 in.
(45.7 x 24.7 x 16.5 cm)
Right: 19 x 10 x 7 3/4 in.
(48.2 x 25.4 x 19.7 cm)
Collection of the artist, Courtesy
Josh Baer Gallery

Above and Below, 1988
metal globestand, books
44 x 61 1/4 x 31 in.
(111.7 x 155.6 x 78.7 cm)
Collection Anne and William
Hokin, Chicago

Domino Theory, 1988
used books
6 1/2 x 70 x 65 in.
(16.5 x 177.8 x 165.1 cm)
Courtesy Studio Guenzani, Milan

Preservation, 1988
velvet cushion, wood table, sheet
music, resin
26 1/2 x 24 1/4 in.
(67.3 x 61.6 cm)
Collection Alice and Marvin
Kosmin, Courtesy Josh Baer
Gallery

Molding Minds, 1989
metal and plaster objects, wood
pedestal
41 1/2 x 48 x 16 in.
(105.4 x 121.9 x 40.6 cm)
Collection Ronnie and Samuel
Heyman, New York

JUAN MUÑOZ
Dragon Back, 1990
mixed media
Courtesy Lisson Gallery, London

JULIAN OPIE
Night Light 14/3343CC, 1989
rubber, aluminum, glass, plastic,
wood, stainless steel, fluorescent
light, cellulose paint
73 1/2 x 48 x 17 in.
(188 x 123 x 43 cm)
Courtesy Lisson Gallery, London

Night Light 24/1343BY, 1989
wood, glass, rubber, aluminum,
cellulose paint, fluorescent light,
galvanized steel
72 3/4 x 48 1/2 x 15 3/4 in.
(186 x 124 x 40 cm)
Courtesy Lisson Gallery, London

Night Light 20/2222GY, 1989
rubber, aluminum, glass, plastic,
wood, stainless steel, fluorescent
light
73 1/2 x 48 x 15 3/4 in.
(188 x 123 x 40 cm)
Courtesy Lisson Gallery, London

Night Light 16/2222CC, 1989
rubber, aluminum, glass, plastic,
wood, stainless steel, fluorescent
light, cellulose paint
72 3/4 x 48 1/2 x 15 3/4 in.
(186 x 124 x 40 cm)
Courtesy Lisson Gallery, London

Night Light 22/3333CY, 1989
wood, glass, rubber, aluminum,
cellulose paint, fluorescent light,
plastic
72 3/4 x 48 1/2 x 17 in.
(186 x 124 x 43 cm)
Courtesy Lisson Gallery, London

Night Light 19/1343GY, 1989
rubber, aluminum, glass, plastic,
wood, stainless steel, fluorescent
light, cellulose paint
73 x 48 x 17 3/4 in.
(187 x 123 x 45 cm)
Courtesy Lisson Gallery, London

Night Light 21/2222BB, 1989
rubber, aluminum, glass, plastic,
wood, stainless steel, fluorescent
light
73 1/2 x 48 x 15 3/4 in.
(188 x 123 x 40 cm)
Courtesy Lisson Gallery, London

Night Light 25/3333CB, 1989
wood, glass, rubber, aluminum,
cellulose paint, fluorescent light,
plastic
72 3/4 x 48 1/2 x 16 1/2 in.
(186 x 124 x 42 cm)
Courtesy Lisson Gallery, London

Night Light 26/5444CY, 1989
wood, glass, rubber, anodized
aluminum, zincoid, fluorescent
light
72 3/4 x 48 1/2 x 15 3/4 in.
(186 x 124 x 40 cm)
Courtesy Lisson Gallery, London

HAIM STEINBACH
Untitled (daybed, coffin), 1989
mixed media construction
71 x 102 1/2 x 82 in.
(180.3 x 260.3 x 208.3 cm)
Courtesy Sonnabend Gallery, New
York, and Jay Gorney Modern
Art, New York

EXHIBITION HISTORIES

GRENVILLE DAVEY

1961 Born Launceston, Cornwall, England

1981- Studied Exeter College of Art and

1985 Design at Goldsmiths College, B.A. Fine Arts

SOLO EXHIBITIONS

1988 Lisson Gallery, London (also 1987)

SELECTED GROUP EXHIBITIONS

1989 *Ateliers en liberté, 1989, Aspects de la jeune sculpture européenne*, Fondation Cartier, Paris
Lia Rumma, Naples
Prospect '89, Frankfurter Kunstverein, Frankfurt
Melencolia, Galerie Grita Insam, Vienna

1988 *1988*, Centre National d'Art Contemporain, Grenoble
Aperto, Venice Biennale, Venice
John Gibson, New York

1986 Showroom Gallery, London

KATHARINA FRITSCH

1956 Born Essen, West Germany

1977 Kunstakademie Düsseldorf

1981 Studied with Professor Fritz Schwegler

SOLO EXHIBITIONS

1989 Kunstverein Münster, Munster
Portikus, Frankfurt
Westfälischer Kunstverein, Munich

1988 Kunsthalle Basel, Basel, Switzerland
Institute of Contemporary Art, London

1987 Kaiser Wilhelm Museum, Krefeld

1985 Galerie Johnen & Schöttle, Cologne
Galerie Schneider, Konstanz, Switzerland

1984 Galerie Rüdiger Schöttle, Munich

SELECTED GROUP EXHIBITIONS

1989 Stichting De Appel, Amsterdam
What is Contemporary Art?, Rooseum, Malmö, Sweden

1988 *Cultural Geometry*, Deste Foundation for Contemporary Art, House of Cyprus, Athens, Greece
Collections pour une région, capc Musée d'art contemporain, Bordeaux
Galerie Johnen & Schöttle, Cologne
Biennial, Sydney, Australia
The Binational: German Art of the Late 80's, Städtische Kunsthalle, Kunstsammlung Nordrhein-Westfalen, and Kunstverein für die Rheinlande und Westfalen, Düsseldorf (traveled to Boston)
Carnegie International, The Carnegie Museum of Art, Pittsburgh

1987 *Anderer Leute Kunst*, Museum Haus Lange, Krefeld
Skulptur Projekte Münster, Munster
Bestiarium, Galerie Rüdiger Schöttle, Munich
Multiples, Galerie Daniel Buchholz, Cologne
The Ydessa Gallery, Toronto

1986 *Von Raum zu Raum*, Kunstverein Hamburg, Hamburg
Sonsbeek '86, Arnheim, West Germany
Aus den Anfngen, Kunstfonds, Bonn
Europa/America, Museum Ludwig, Cologne
Junge Rheinische Kunst, Galerie Schipka, Sofia
A Distanced View, The New Museum of Contemporary Art, New York

ROBERT GOBER

1954 Born Wallingford, Connecticut

1976 B.A., Middlebury College, Connecticut

SOLO EXHIBITIONS

1989 Paula Cooper Gallery, New York (also 1987, 1985, and 1984)

1988 Tyler School of Art, Temple University, Elkins Park, Pennsylvania
Art Institute of Chicago, Chicago

1987 Galerie Jean Bernier, Athens, Greece

1986 Daniel Weinberg Gallery, Los Angeles (also 1985)

SELECTED GROUP EXHIBITIONS

1989 *Filling in the Gap*, Richard L. Feigen, Chicago
Pre/Pop Post/Appropriation, Stux Gallery, New York
Three Decades: The Oliver-Hoffmann Collection, Museum of Contemporary Art, Chicago

1988 *Furniture as Art*, Museum Boyman-van Beuningen, Rotterdam, Holland
Real Inventions/Invented Functions, Laurie Rubin Gallery, New York
Sculpture Parallels, Sidney Janis Gallery, New York
Robert Gober, Christopher Wool, 303 Gallery, New York
LXIII Biennale di Venezia, Venice
Utopia Post Utopia: Configurations of Nature and Culture in Recent Sculpture and Photography, Institute of Contemporary Art, Boston

1987 *The Great Drawing Show 1587-1987*, Michael Kohn Gallery, Los Angeles
Artists from Paula Cooper Gallery, Galeria EMI Valentin de Carvalho, Lisbon
Extreme Order, Lia Rumma, Naples
Crousel-Hussenot, Paris
Art Against AIDS: A Benefit Exhibition, Paula Cooper Gallery, New York
NY Art Now: The Saatchi Collection, The Saatchi Collection, London
Avant-Garde in the Eighties, Los Angeles County Museum of Art, Los Angeles

One Hand Clapping, Karsten Schubert, Ltd., London

1986 *Robert Gober, Jeff Koons, Peter Nadin, Meyer Vaisman*, Jay Gorney Modern Art, New York
Drawing, Knight Gallery, Charlotte, North Carolina
Objects From the Modern World, Daniel Weinberg Gallery, Los Angeles
Robert Gober/Kevin Larmon: An Installation, Nature Morte, New York
New Sculpture: Robert Gober, Jeff Koons, Haim Steinbach, The Renaissance Society at The University of Chicago, Chicago
Paula Cooper Gallery, New York (four shows)
Robert Gober, Nancy Shaver, Alan Turner, Meg Webster, Cable Gallery, New York
Works from the Paula Cooper Gallery, John Berggruen Gallery, San Francisco
Art on Paper Exhibition, Weatherspoon Art Gallery, The University of North Carolina at Greensboro
Galerie Max Hetzler, Cologne
Art for Young Collectors, The Renaissance Society at The University of Chicago, Chicago

Drawings, Gallery Casas, Toledo Oosterom, New York
Art and Its Double: Recent Developments in New York Art, Fundació Caixa de Pensions, Barcelona and Madrid (traveled)
1976-1986: Ten Years of Collecting Contemporary Art (Selections from the Edward R. Downe, Jr. Collection), Wellesley College Museum, Wellesley, Massachusetts

1985 Paula Cooper Gallery, New York (two shows)
AIDS Benefit Exhibition, Daniel Weinberg Gallery, Los Angeles
Scapes, University Art Museum, University of California, Santa Barbara (traveled)
Benefit for The Kitchen, Brooke Alexander, New York

1984 PS 122 Gallery, New York
Paula Cooper Gallery, New York
Jus de Pomme, New York

1983 *New York Work*, Studio 10, Chur, Switzerland
Barbara Toll Fine Arts, New York

1982 Paula Cooper Gallery, New York (two shows)

1981 *Three Look Into American Homelife*, Ian Birksted Gallery, New York

JEFF KOONS

1955 Born York, Pennsylvania
1976 B.F.A., Maryland Institute College of Art, Baltimore

SOLO EXHIBITIONS

1989 *Jeff Koons—Nieuw Werk*, Galerie 't Venster and Rotterdamse Kunststichting, Rotterdam
1988 Museum of Contemporary Art, Chicago
Sonnabend Gallery, New York
Galerie Max Hetzler, Cologne
Donald Young Gallery, Chicago

1987 Daniel Weinberg Gallery, Los Angeles
1986 International With Monument Gallery, New York (also 1985)
1985 Feature, Chicago

SELECTED GROUP EXHIBITIONS

1989 *Horn of Plenty*, Stedelijk Museum, Amsterdam

Conspicuous Display, Stedman Art Gallery, Rutgers University, Camden, New Jersey
Whitney Biennial, Whitney Museum of American Art, New York
Suburban Home Life: Tracking the American Dream, Whitney Museum at Federal Plaza, New York

A Forest of Signs: Art in the Crisis of Representation, Museum of Contemporary Art, Los Angeles
The Silent Baroque, Galerie Thaddaeus Ropac at the Villa Arenberg, Salzburg, Austria

1988 *Cultural Geometry*, Deste Foundation for Contemporary Art, House of Cyprus, Athens, Greece
Schlaf der Vernunft, Museum Fridericianum, Kassel
Redefining the Object, University Art Galleries, Wright State University, Dayton, Ohio
New York in View, Kunstverein München, Munich
Collection pour une région, capc Musée d'art contemporain, Bordeaux
NY Art Now—Part II, The Saatchi Collection, London
Artschwager: His Peers and Persuasion, 1963-1988, Daniel Weinberg Gallery, Los Angeles, and Leo Castelli Gallery, New York
Colección Sonnabend, Centro de Arte Reina Sofia, Madrid, and capc Musée d'art contemporain, Bordeaux
Sculpture Parallels, Sidney Janis Gallery, New York
Altered States, Kent Fine Art, New York
Art at the End of the Social, Rooseum, Malmö, Sweden
Works-Concepts-Processes-Situations-Information, Ausstellungsraum Hans Meyer, Düsseldorf
New Works, Daniel Weinberg Gallery, Los Angeles

The Binational: American Art of the Late 80's, The Institute of Contemporary Art and The Museum of Fine Arts, Boston (traveled to Germany)
Three Decades: The Oliver-Hoffmann Collection, The Museum of Contemporary Art, Chicago
Carnegie International, The Carnegie Museum of Art, Pittsburgh

1987 *Whitney Biennial*, Whitney Museum of American Art, New York
Les courtiers du désir, Galeries Contemporaines, Centre Georges Pompidou, Paris
New York New, Galerie Paul Maenz, Cologne
Avant-Garde in the Eighties, Los Angeles County Museum of Art, Los Angeles
Skulptur Projekte Münster, Munster
Romance, Knight Gallery, Charlotte, North Carolina
Post-Abstract Abstraction, The Aldrich Museum of Contemporary Art, Ridgefield, Connecticut

1986 *Admired Work*, John Weber Gallery, New York
Jay Gorney Modern Art, New York
Objects from the Modern World, Daniel Weinberg Gallery, Los Angeles
Time After Time, Diane Brown Gallery, New York
Spiritual America, CEPA Galleries, Buffalo, New York
Damaged Goods: Desire and the Economy of The Object, The New Museum of Contemporary Art, New York
Otis/Parsons Art Gallery, Los Angeles

Paravision, Margo Leavin Gallery, Los Angeles
Donald Young Gallery, Chicago
Endgame: Reference and Simulation in Recent Painting and Sculpture, Institute of Contemporary Art, Boston
Art and Its Double: Recent Developments in New York Art, Fundació Caixa de Pensions, Barcelona and Madrid
Sonnabend Gallery, New York
Galerie Max Hetzler, Cologne
New Sculpture: Robert Gober, Jeff Koons, Haim Steinbach, The Renaissance Society at The University of Chicago, Chicago
Europa/America, Museum Ludwig, Cologne
Modern Objects, A New Dawn, Baskerville & Watson, New York

1985 *Objects in Collision*, The Kitchen, New York
International With Monument Gallery, New York
Logosimuli, Daniel Newburg Gallery, New York
Affiliations: Recent Sculpture and Its Antecedents, Whitney Museum of American Art at Stamford, Connecticut
New Ground, Luhring, Augustine & Hodes Gallery, New York
Post Production, Feature, Chicago
Signs II, Michael Klein, Inc., New York
Cult and Decorum, Tibor de Nagy Gallery, New York
New Ground, Luhring, Augustine & Hodes Gallery, New York
Galerie Crousel-Hussenot, Paris
303 Gallery, New York

ANNETTE LEMIEUX

1957 Born Norfolk, Virginia
1980 B.F.A., Hartford Art School,
University of Hartford,
Connecticut

SOLO EXHIBITIONS

1989 Josh Baer Gallery, New York (also
1987)
The John and Mable Ringling
Museum, Sarasota, Florida
Center for the Fine Arts, Miami,
Florida
1988 Lisson Gallery, London
Rhona Hoffman Gallery, Chicago
Matrix Gallery, Wadsworth
Atheneum, Hartford, Connecticut
1987 Cash/Newhouse, New York (also
1986, 1984)
Daniel Weinberg Gallery,
Los Angeles
1984 Artists Space, New York

SELECTED GROUP EXHIBITIONS

1989 *Pre/Pop Post/Appropriation*, Stux
Gallery, New York
Revamp, Review, International
Center for Photography at
Woodstock, Woodstock, New York
Prospect '89, Schirn Kunsthalle,
Frankfurt
INFAS: 7 Artists, The Space,
Hanae Mori Foundation, Tokyo
Drawing to a Close, Daniel
Weinberg Gallery, Los Angeles
Painting/Object/Photograph,
Barbara Krakow Gallery, Boston
The Silent Baroque, Galerie
Thaddeus Ropac at the Villa
Arenberg, Salzburg, Austria

*The Photography of Invention—
American Pictures of the 1980s*,
National Museum of American
Art, Smithsonian Institution,
Washington, D.C.
*10 + 10: Contemporary Soviet and
American Painters*, Modern Art
Museum of Fort Worth (traveled)
*Contemporary Perspectives 1:
Abstraction in Question*, The John
and Mable Ringling Museum of
Art, Sarasota, Florida, and the
Center for the Fine Arts, Miami
Les États Généraux, Galerie
Montenay, Paris
1988 *Cultural Geometry*, Deste Founda-
tion for Contemporary Art,
House of Cyprus, Athens, Greece
Media Post Media, Scott Hanson
Gallery, New York
The Return of the Hero, Burden
Gallery, Aperture Foundation,
New York
Photography on the Edge, Patrick
and Beatrice Haggerty Museum
of Art, Marquette University,
Milwaukee
*Artschwager, His Peers and Per-
suasion, 1963-1988*, Daniel
Weinberg Gallery, Los Angeles,
and Leo Castelli Gallery,
New York
Altered States, Kent Fine Art,
New York
Reprises de Vues, Halle Sud,
Geneva
Sculpture, Brooke Alexander,
New York
Objects, Lorence-Monk, New York
Art at the End of the Social,
Rooseum, Malmö, Sweden
New Work, Josh Baer Gallery,
New York
*The Binational: American Art of
the Late 80's*, The Institute of
Contemporary Art and The
Museum of Fine Arts, Boston
(traveled to Germany)

*Hybrid Neutral: Modes of Abstrac-
tion and the Social*, The University
of North Texas Art Gallery, Denton
(traveled)
Fuller Gross Gallery, San Francisco
1987 Annina Nosei Gallery, New York
The Antique Future, Massimo
Audiello Gallery, New York
Whitney Biennial, Whitney
Museum of American Art,
New York
Extreme Order, Lia Rumma,
Naples
Fake, The New Museum of Con-
temporary Art, New York
Lawrence Oliver Gallery,
Philadelphia
Beyond the Image, First Street
Forum, St. Louis
Romance, Knight Gallery,
Charlotte, North Carolina
Subtext, Kent Fine Art, New York
of Ever-Ever Land i speak, Stux
Gallery, New York
International With Monument,
New York
Tom Cugliani, New York
Pat Hearn Gallery, New York
Collección Sonnabend, Centro
d'Arte Reina Sofia, Ministerio de
Cultura, Madrid
*Currents 12: Simulations, New
American Conceptualism*,
Milwaukee Art Museum,
Milwaukee
*Recent Tendencies in Black and
White*, Sidney Janis Gallery,
New York
The Beauty of Circumstance, Josh
Baer Gallery, New York

1986   Cash/Newhouse, New York (also
        1985)
        Cleveland Institute of Contem-
        porary Art, Cleveland
        Metro Pictures, New York (also
        1984)
        Currents, Institute of Contem-
        porary Art, Boston
        Time After Time, Diane Brown
        Gallery, New York
        Altered States, Proctor Art Center,
        Bard College, Annendale-on-
        Hudson, New York

Spiritual America, CEPA Galleries,
Buffalo, New York
Luhring, Augustine & Hodes
Gallery, New York
Rhona Hoffman Gallery, Chicago
Brooke Alexander, New York
Ultrasurd, S. L. Simpson Gallery,
Toronto
Modern Sleep, American Fine
Arts Co., New York

1985   *57th Street between A&D*, Holly
        Solomon Gallery, New York
        Past and Future Perfect, Hallwalls,
        Buffalo, New York
        303 Gallery, New York
        Michael Bennett Gallery, New York
        *A Brave New World, A New
        Generation: 40 New York Artists*,
        Udstillingsbygning Ved
        Charlottenborg, Copenhagen,
        Denmark, and Lund Kunsthalle,
        Lund, Sweden

JUAN MUÑOZ

1953   Born Madrid, Spain
1979   Central School of Art and
        Design, London
        Crydon School of Art and
        Technology, London
1982   Pratt Institute, New York

SOLO EXHIBITIONS

1989   Lisson Gallery, London (also
        1987)
1988   Galeria Jean Bernier, Athens,
        Greece
        Galerie Konrad Fischer,
        Düsseldorf
        Galerie Ghislaine Hussenot, Paris
1987   Galerie Roger Pailhas, Marseille
        Galeria Cómicos, Lisbon (also
        1985)
1986   Galerie Joost Declercq, Gent
        Galería Marga Paz, Madrid
1984   Galería Fernando Vijande,
        Madrid

SELECTED GROUP EXHIBITIONS

1989   *Theatergarden Bestearium*,
        Institute for Art and Urban
        Resources, P.S.1, New York
        Magiciens de la terre, Musée
        national d'art moderne, Centre
        Georges Pompidou, Paris
1988   *Jan de Pavert y Juan Muñoz*, Arte
        y Amicitia, Amsterdam
        Steirischer Herbst 88, Grazer
        Kunstverein, Graz, Austria
1987   *Lili Dujourie/Juan Muñoz*, FRAC
        des Pays de la Loire, Abbaye de
        Fontevraud, France
        *Cristina Iglesias, Juan Muñoz,
        Susana Solano*, capc Musée d'art
        contemporain, Bordeaux
        Dynamiques et Interrogations,
        ARC, Paris
1986   *Chambres d'Amis*, Museum van
        Hedendaagse Kunst, Gent
        *1981-1986. Pintores y Escultores
        Españoles*, Fundación Caja de
        Pensiones, Madrid
        *Aperto 86, Cuatro Artistas
        Españoles*, Biennale di Venezia,
        Venice

*Ateliers Internationaux des Pays
de la Loire*, Fondation nationale
des arts graphiques et plastiques,
Abbaye de Fontevraud, France
1985   *V Salón de los 16*, Museo Español
        de Arte Contemporáneo, Madrid
        Stedelijk Van Abbemuseum,
        Eindhoven, Holland
1983   *La Imagen del Animal*, Casa del
        Monte, Madrid
        Seis Españoles en Madrid, Galería
        Fernando Vijande, Madrid
1982   Büro, Berlin
1981   Friart, Freiburg
        Institute for Art and Urban
        Resources P.S.1, New York,
        Room 202

JULIAN OPIE

1958	Born London, England
1979-	Goldsmith's School of Art,
1982	London

SOLO EXHIBITIONS

1988	Lisson Gallery, London (also 1986 and 1983)
1986	Franco Tosselli Gallery, Milan
1985	Groninger Museum, Groningen, Holland
	Institute of Contemporary Art, London
1984	*Perspective '84*, Internationale Kunstmesse, Basel, Switzerland, and Kolnischer Kunstverein, Cologne

GROUP EXHIBITIONS

| 1989 | *Filling in the Gap*, Richard L. Feigen, Chicago |
| 1988 | *Britannica: Trente Ans de Sculpture*, Musée des Beaux Arts Andre Malraux, Le Havre (traveled) |

1988	*Les Années 80: À la Surface de la Peinture*, Centre d'art contemporain, Abbaye Saint-Andre, Meymac, France
	Wolff Gallery, New York
1987	*British Art of the 1980's: 1987*, organized by the British Council (traveled)
1986	*Focus on the Image: Selection from the Rivendell Collection*, The Art Museum Association of America, San Francisco (traveled)
1986	*Forty Years of Modern Art 1945-85*, Tate Gallery, London
	Sculpture—9 Artists from Britain, Louisiana Museum, Humlebaek, Denmark
	XVII Triennale de Milano (Lucio Amelio, Terr Morta), Milan, and Grand Palais, Paris
	De Sculptura-Junge Bildhauer 1986, Wiener Festwochen, Vienna
	Englische Bildhauer, Galerie Harald Behm, Hamburg

	Prospect 86, Frankfurter Kunstverein, Frankfurt
	Correspondence Europe, Stedelijk Museum, Amsterdam
1985	*Still-Life: A New Life*, Harris Museum and Art Gallery, Preson (traveled)
	Anniottanta, Assessorato alla Cultura del Commune di Ravenna, Bologna, Italy (traveled)
	Three British Sculptors, The Israel Museum, Jerusalem
	Place Saint Lambert Investigations, Éspace Nord, Liège, Belgium
	Figure 1, Aberystwyth Arts Centre, Wales
	The Irresistible Object-Still Life 1600-1985, Leeds City Art Galleries, Leeds, England

HAIM STEINBACH

1944	Born Israel, U.S. citizen, 1962
1971-	M.F.A., Yale University, New
1973	Haven, Connecticut
1962-	B.F.A., Pratt Institute, Brooklyn,
1968	New York

SOLO EXHIBITIONS

1989	Margo Leavin Gallery, Los Angeles
	Galerie Roger Pailhas, Marseille
	Yvon Lambert, Paris
1988	capc Musée d'art contemporain, Bordeaux
	Jay Gorney Modern Art, New York (also 1986)
	Gruppo GFT, Pier 88, New York

1987	Lia Rumma, Naples
	Rhona Hoffman Gallery, Chicago
	Sonnabend Gallery and Jay Gorney Modern Art, New York
1986	Washington Project for the Arts, Washington, D.C.
1985	Cable Gallery, New York
1983	Graduate Center Mall, City University, New York, collaboration with Julie Wachtel
1982	Concord Gallery, New York
1981	Washington Project for the Arts, Washington, D.C., collaboration with Johanna Boyce
	Berkshire Community College, Pittsfield, Massachusetts

SELECTED GROUP EXHIBITIONS

1989	*Selections from the Collection of Marc and Livia Straus*, The Aldrich Museum of Contemporary Art, Ridgefield, Connecticut
	What is Contemporary Art?, Rooseum, Malmö, Sweden
	Complex Object, Galería Marga Paz, Madrid
	Langer & Co., New York

Horn of Plenty, Stedelijk
Museum, Amsterdam
*Natura Naturata, An Argument
for Still-Life*, Josh Baer Gallery,
New York
Abstraction in Question, The John
and Mable Ringling Museum of
Art, Sarasota, Florida
Oberlin College, Oberlin, Ohio
*A Forest of Signs: Art in the Crisis
of Representation*, Museum of
Contemporary Art, Los Angeles
Repetition, Hirschl & Adler
Modern, New York
Microsculpture, University of
Rhode Island, Kingston
Conspicuous Display, Stedman
Art Gallery, Rutgers University,
Camden, New Jersey
*Three Decades: The Oliver-
Hoffmann Collection*, Museum of
Contemporary Art, Chicago

1988 *New Urban Landscape*, The
World Financial Center, New York
*Innovations in Sculpture
1985-1988*, The Aldrich Museum
of Contemporary Art, Ridgefield,
Connecticut
*Works-Concepts-Processes-
Situations-Information*, Galerie
Hans Mayer, Düsseldorf
*The Binational: American Art of
the Late 80's*, The Institute of
Contemporary Art and The
Museum of Fine Arts, Boston
(traveled to Germany)
Art at the End of the Social,
Rooseum, Malmö, Sweden
Colleción Sonnabend, Reina
Sofia-Centro de Arte Contem-
poráneo, Madrid (traveled)

*The Pop Project: Part IV, Nostalgia
as Resistance*, Clocktower, The
Institute for Art and Urban
Resources, New York
A "Drawing" Show, Cable
Gallery, New York
Hover Culture, Metro Pictures,
New York
Collections pour une région, capc
Musée d'art contemporain,
Bordeaux
Metamorphosis of the Object, The
Israel Museum, Jerusalem
*Artschwager: His Peers and Per-
suasion, 1963-1988*, Daniel
Weinberg Gallery, Los Angeles,
and Leo Castelli Gallery, New York
New York in View, Kunstverein
München, Munich
Sculpture Parallels, Sidney Janis
Gallery, New York
ReDefining the Object, University
Art Galleries, Wright State
University, Dayton, Ohio
(traveled)
The Return of the Hero, Burden
Gallery, Aperture Foundation,
New York
Schlaf der Vernunft, Museum
Fridericianum, Kassel
Broken Neon, Galerie Dürr,
Munich
Cultural Geometry, Deste Founda-
tion for Contemporary Art,
House of Cyprus, Athens, Greece
Common Thread, Daniel
Weinberg Gallery, Los Angeles,
and Leo Castelli Gallery, New York

1987 *Primary Structures*, Rhona
Hoffman Gallery, Chicago
*NY Art Now, The Saatchi Collec-
tion*, The Saatchi Collection,
London
One Hand Clapping, Karsten
Schubert, Ltd, London
The Castle, an installation by
Group Material, Documenta 8,
Kassel
Romance, Knight Gallery, Charlotte,
North Carolina
New York New, Galerie Paul
Maenz, Cologne
Art Against AIDS, Jay Gorney
Modern Art and Paula Cooper
Gallery, New York
Extreme Order, Lia Rumma,
Naples
Les courtiers du désir, Galeries
Contemporaines, Centre Georges
Pompidou, Paris
Avant-Garde in the Eighties, Los
Angeles County Museum of Art,
Los Angeles
Reconstruct, John Gibson,
New York
Perverted By Language, Hillwood
Gallery, Long Island University,
Greenvale, New York
Tenth Anniversary Benefit Auction,
The New Museum of Contem-
porary Art, New York
Margo Leavin Gallery, Los Angeles
New York Now, The Israel
Museum, Jerusalem
*Currents 12: Simulations, New
American Conceptualism*,
Milwaukee Art Museum,
Milwaukee
The Transformative Vision,
Davis/McClain Gallery, Houston
Industrial Icons, University Art
Gallery, California State University,
San Diego

1986   *Post Pop Art*, Michael Kohn
Gallery, Los Angeles
*New Sculpture: Robert Gober, Jeff
Koons, Haim Steinbach*, The
Renaissance Society at The
University of Chicago, Chicago
Jay Gorney Modern Art, New York
Carpenter & Hochman, New York
Art & Leisure, The Kitchen,
New York
The Color Red, Massimo Audiello,
New York
Cable Gallery, New York
*Damaged Goods: Desire and the
Economy of The Object*, New
Museum of Contemporary Art,
New York
Rooted Rhetoric, Castele Dell'Ovo,
Naples
Paravision 2, Margo Leavin
Gallery, Los Angeles
The Brokerage of Desire, Otis Art
Institute, Los Angeles
Donald Young Gallery, Chicago
*Endgame: Reference and Simula-
tion in Recent Painting and
Sculpture*, Institute of Contem-
porary Art, Boston
*Art and Its Double: Recent
Developments in New York Art*,
Fundació Caixa de Pensions,
Barcelona and Madrid
Bard College, New York
New New York, Cleveland Center
for the Contemporary Arts,
Cleveland
*Seven Wonderful Children We
Have Never Seen*, performance
collaboration with Pery Hober-
man, The Kitchen, New York
Time After Time, Diane Brown
Gallery, New York
Postmasters Gallery, New York

1985   Michael Kohn Gallery, Los Angeles
Jay Gorney Modern Art, New York
Cult and Decorum, Tibor de
Nagy Gallery, New York
Post Production, Feature, Chicago
Nature Morte, New York
Objects in Collision, The Kitchen,
New York
Infotainment, Rhona Hoffman
Gallery, Chicago (organized by
Livet Reichard Co., Inc., New
York, traveled)

SELECTED BIBLIOGRAPHY

GENERAL

BOOKS

Foster, Hal, ed. *The Anti-Aesthetic: Essays on Postmodern Culture*. Port Townsend, Washington: Bay Press, 1983.

———. *Recodings: Art, Spectacle, Cultural Politics*. Port Townsend, Washington: Bay Press, 1985.

Wallis, Brian, ed. *Art After Modernism: Rethinking Representation*. New York and Boston: The New Museum of Contemporary Art and David R. Godine, Publisher, Inc., 1984.

CATALOGS

Abstraction in Question. Sarasota, Florida: The John and Mable Ringling Museum of Art, 1989. (Gober, Lemieux, Steinbach)

Art at the End of the Social. Malmö, Sweden: Rooseum, 1988. (Gober, Lemieux)

Art Against Aids. New York: American Foundation for AIDS Research, 1987. (Koons, Lemieux, Steinbach)

Art and Its Double: A New York Perspective. Barcelona: Fundació Caixa de Pensions, 1986. (Gober, Koons, Steinbach)

Artschwager: His Peers and Persuasion, 1963-88. Los Angeles and New York: Daniel Weinberg Gallery and Leo Castelli Gallery, 1988. (Lemieux, Steinbach)

Avant-Garde in the Eighties. Los Angeles: Los Angeles County Museum of Art, 1987. (Gober, Koons, Steinbach)

The Binational: American and German Art of the Late 80's. Boston: The Institute of Contemporary Art and the Museum of Fine Arts; Cologne: DuMont Buchverlag, 1988. 2 vol. (Fritsch, Gober, Koons, Lemieux, Steinbach)

A Brokerage of Desire. Los Angeles: Otis Art Institute of Parsons School of Design, 1986. (Koons, Steinbach)

Cultural Geometry. Athens: Deste Foundation for Contemporary Art, 1988. (Gober, Lemieux, Steinbach)

Currents 12: Simulation, New American Conceptualism. Milwaukee: Milwaukee Art Museum, 1987. (Koons, Lemieux, Steinbach)

Damaged Goods: Desire and the Economy of the Object. New York: The New Museum of Contemporary Art, 1986. (Koons, Steinbach)

Endgame: Reference and Simulation in Recent Painting and Sculpture. Boston and Cambridge: Institute of Contemporary Art and MIT Press, 1987. (Koons, Steinbach)

Fake. New York: The New Museum of Contemporary Art, 1987. (Lemieux, Steinbach)

A Forest of Signs: Art in the Crisis of Representation. Los Angeles: Museum of Contemporary Art, 1989. (Koons, Steinbach)

Günther Förg, Robert Gober, Axel Hutte, Jon Kessler, Hubert Kiecol, Jeff Koons, Meuser, Heimo Zobernig. Cologne: Galerie Max Hetzler, 1986. (Gober, Koons)

Horn of Plenty: Sixteen Artists from NYC. Amsterdam: Stedelijk Museum, 1989. (Gober, Koons, Steinbach)

New Sculpture: Robert Gober, Jeff Koons, Haim Steinbach. Chicago: The Renaissance Society at the University of Chicago, 1986. (Gober, Koons, Steinbach)

New York Art Now. Jerusalem: The Israel Museum, 1987. (Gober, Koons, Steinbach)

New York in View. Munich: Kunstverein München, 1988. (Koons, Steinbach)

Post-Abstract Abstraction. Ridgefield, Connecticut: The Aldrich Museum of Contemporary Art, 1987. (Koons, Steinbach)

Pre-Pop Post-Appropriation. New York: Stux Gallery, 1989. (Gober, Lemieux)

Three Decades: The Oliver-Hoffmann Collection. Chicago: Museum of Contemporary Art, 1989. (Gober, Koons, Steinbach)

Utopia Post Utopia: Configurations of Nature and Culture in Recent Sculpture and Photography. Boston and Cambridge: Institute of Contemporary Art and MIT Press, 1988. (Gober, Koons, Lemieux)

ARTICLES

Cameron, Dan. "Art and Its Double: A New York Perspective." *Flash Art*, May 1987, pp. 57-71. (Gober, Koons, Steinbach)

Christov-Bakargiev, Carolyn. "Something Nowhere: The Mute Statement of Recent Sculpture Attempts to Formulate a Possible Self." *Flash Art*, May/June 1988, p. 81. (Fritsch, Muñoz)

Collins, Tricia, and Milazzo, Richard. "Radical Consumption and the New Poverty." *New Observations*, October 1987, p. 6. (Koons, Lemieux)

———. "Spiritual America." *CEPA Quarterly*, Spring 1986, pp. 4-8. (Koons, Lemieux)

Cone, Michele. "Ready Mades on the Couch." *Artscribe International*, June/July 1986, pp. 30-33. (Gober, Koons)

Faust, Wolfgang Max. "Now New York New." *Wolkenkratzer*, January/February 1988, pp. 20-25. (Gober, Koons)

Heartney, Eleanor. "Neo-Geo Storms New York." *New Art Examiner*, September 1986, pp. 26-29. (Koons, Steinbach)

———. "Simulationism, The Hot New Cool Art." *Art News*, January 1987, pp. 130-37. (Koons, Lemieux, Steinbach)

Joselit, David. "Investigating the Ordinary." *Art In America*, May 1988, pp. 148-55. (Gober, Koons, Steinbach)

Kuspit, Donald. "Breakfast of Duchampians." *Contemporanea*, May 1989, pp. 68-72. (Gober, Steinbach)
————. "The Modern Fetish." *Artforum*, October 1988, pp. 132-40. (Steinbach)
Leigh, Christian. "Home Is Where the Heart Is." *Flash Art*, March/April 1989, pp. 79-83. (Gober, Lemieux)

Magnani, Gregorio. "Venice Biennial." *Flash Art*, October 1988, pp. 104-105. (Davey, Gober)
Oliva, Achille Bonito. "Neo America." *Flash Art*, January/February 1988, pp. 62-66. (Lemieux, Steinbach)
Russell, John. "At the Saatchi Collection, A Thin Show of 'NY Art.'" *New York Times*, 3 January 1988, p. C27. (Gober, Koons)

Smith, Roberta. "'80s Art With a Passport to West Germany." *New York Times*, 2 October 1988, p. B33. (Gober, Lemieux)
Taylor, Paul. "Spotlight: Cultural Geometry." *Flash Art*, May/June 1988, pp. 124-25. (Gober, Koons)

GRENVILLE DAVEY

CATALOGS

Grenville Davey. London: Lisson Gallery, 1989.

ARTICLES

Allthorpe-Guyton, Marjorie. *Flash Art*, January/February 1988, p. 128. Review.
Archer, Michael. *Artforum*, January 1988, p. 132. Review.

Kent, Sarah. "Shirazeh Houshiary, Grenville Davey." *Time Out*, 14 October 1987.
Cooke, Lynne. "Object Lessons." *Artscribe International*, September/October 1987, pp. 55-59.
Mercuri, Bernardo. "Young Art: 'Aperto 88,' The Absent Alter Ego." *Tema Celeste*, October/November 1988, pp. 50-52.
Morgan, Stuart. "Cold Comfort." *Artscribe International*, Summer 1988.

————. "Degree Zero: Grenville Davey." *Artscribe International*, January/February 1988, pp. 42-44.
Piguet, Philippe. "Fondation Cartier pour l'art contemporain." *Art Press*, March 1989, p. 66.

KATHARINA FRITSCH

CATALOGS

A Distanced View—The Exhibition (The New Museum of Contemporary Art, New York) as reproduced in *Zien Magazine* 9, 1986, pp. 20-21, 43.
Anderer Leute Kunst. Krefeld: Museum Haus Lange. 1987.
Die intuitive Logik der Katharina Fritsch/The Intuitive Logic of Katharina Fritsch. Basel and London: Kunsthalle Basel; Institute of Contemporary Art, 1988.
Katharina Fritsch. Munich: Westfälischer Kuntverein, 1989.
Katharina Fritsch-Elefant. Krefeld: Kaiser Wilhelm Museum, 1987.
Junge Rheinische Kunst. Sofia: Galerie Schipka, 1986.
Sonsbeek '86. Utrecht, Veen: Reflex, 1986.

Von Hier Aus: Zwei Monate neue Deutsche Kunst in Düsseldorf. Cologne: DuMont, 1984.
Von Raum zu Raum. Hamburg: Kunstverien Hamburg, 1986.

ARTICLES

Blase, Christoph. "On Katharina Fritsch." *Artscribe International*, March/April 1988, pp. 52-55.
Fritsch, Katharina. *"Friedhöfe."* *Kunstforum International*, no. 65, 1983.
Hoffmann, Jörg. "Was macht der Elefant im Museum?" *Neue Westfälische Zeitung*, 16 March 1987.
Locker, Ludwig. "Architektonische Aspekte in der Düsseldorfer Gegenwartskunst." *Artefactum*, March/April 1986.
Koether, Jutta. "Elefant." *Parkett*, no. 13, 1987, pp. 90-92.
————. "Katharina Fritsch, Kaiser Wilhelm Museum." *Artscribe International*, May 1987, p. 84.

————. "A Report from the Field." *Flash Art*, Summer 1988, p. 89.
Ponti, Lisa Licitra. "Il 'progetto scultura' a Münster." *Domus*, September 1987, pp. 110-11.
Puvogel, Renate. "Katharina Fritsch-Elefant." *Kunstforum International*, May/June 1987, pp. 338-40.
Salvioni, Daniel. "Trockel and Fritsch." *Flash Art*, October 1988, p. 110.
Schmidt-Wulffen, Stephan. "Enzyklopädie der Skulptur." *Kunstforum International*, October/November 1987, pp. 288-301.
Wulffen, Thomas. "Katharina Fritsch." *Kunstforum International*, October/November, pp. 168-73.

ROBERT GOBER

CATALOGS

Artistas da Paula Cooper Gallery. Lisbon: Galeria EMI Valentim de Carvalho, 1987.

Biennial 1989. New York: Whitney Museum of American Art, 1989.

Extreme Order. Naples: Lia Rumma Gallery, 1987.

Furniture as Art. Rotterdam: Museum Boymans-van Beuningen, 1988.

Il luogo degli artisti: XLIII esposizione d'arte, La Biennale di Venezia. Milan: La Biennale and Fabbri, 1988.

Robert Gober. Elkins Park: Temple University and Tyler School of Art, 1988.

Robert Gober. Athens: Jean Bernier Gallery, 1987.

Sculpture Inside/Outside. Minneapolis: Walker Art Center, 1988.

Scapes. Santa Barbara: University Art Museum, University of California, Santa Barbara, 1985.

ARTICLES

Allthorpe-Guyton, Marjorie. "NY Art Now: The Saatchi Collection, London." *Flash Art*, November/December 1987, p. 109.

Beaumont, Mary Rose. "Eleven Artists from Paula Cooper." *Arts Review*, 3 June 1988.

Berman, Ann E. "Sculptors-in-Progress." *Town and Country*, September 1987, pp. 269-70.

Beyer, Lucie. "Förg, Kiecol, Meuser, Hutte, Zobernig, Koons, Kessler, Gober." *Flash Art*, February/March 1987.

Boodro, Michael. "Art Takes Shape." *HG*, May 1988, p. 35.

Boone, Susan. "The Finishing Touch." *Home*, December 1988, p. 78.

Brenson, Michael. "Coming to Grips with Contemporary Sculpture." *New York Times*, 19 June 1988, p. C33.

Campitelli, Maria. "Robert Gober." *Juliet, December 1988/January 1989*, p. 35.

Collins, Tricia, and Milazzo, Richard. "Robert Gober: The Subliminal Function of Sinks." *Kunstforum International*, June/August 1986, pp. 56-57.

Cooke, Lynne. "Aperto Ma Non Troppo." *Art International*, Autumn 1988, p. 61.

Decter, Joshua. "Robert Gober." *Arts Magazine*, December 1985, p. 124.

Evans, Steven. "Robert Gober/Christopher Wool." *Artscribe International*, November/December 1988, p. 80.

Gardner, Paul. "Collecting Art of the Eighties." *Contemporanea*, September/October 1988, p. 58.

Indiana, Gary. "The Torture Garden." *Village Voice*, 17 October 1987, p. 105.

Juarez, Roberto. "Selected Similarities." *Bomb*, Winter 1987, p. 84.

Koether, Jutta. "Robert Gober." *Artforum*, February 1989, p. 145.

———. "Group Show, Max Hetzler." *Artscribe International*, March/April 1987, pp. 91-92.

Leigh, Christian. "Into the Blue." *Art & Auction*, May 1989, pp. 264-67.

Mahoney, Robert. "Real Inventions/Invented Functions." *Arts Magazine*, May 1988, p. 102.

Marincola, Paula. "Robert Gober, Tyler School of Art Gallery." *Artforum*, May 1988, p. 153.

Morgan, Robert C. "New York in Review." *Arts Magazine*, May 1989, p. 112.

Nickas, Robert, and Power, Kevin. "Art and Its Double." *Flash Art*, February/March 1987, pp. 113-14.

Perez, Luis Francisco. "El Arte y su Doble." *Tema Celeste*, April/June 1987, pp. 66-67.

Pincus-Witten, Robert. "Electrostatic Cling or the Massacre of Innocence." *Artscribe International*, Summer 1987, pp. 36-43.

Phillips, Dennis. "Tre Poesie." *Spazio Umano*, January 1989, pp. 81-86.

Princenthal, Nancy. "Robert Gober at Paula Cooper." *Art in America*, December 1987, pp. 153-54.

Puvogel, Renate. "Robert Gober at Galerie Hetzler, Galerie Gisela Capitain." *Artscribe International*, May 1989.

Rian, Jeffrey. "Past Sense, Present Sense." *Artscribe International*, January/February 1989, pp. 60-65.

Rinder, Larry. "Kevin Larmon and Robert Gober." *Flash Art*, May/June 1986, pp. 56-57.

Rubinstein, Meyer Raphael, and Daniel Weiner. "Spotlight: Robert Gober." *Flash Art*, January/February 1988, p. 119.

Russell, John. "Robert Gober at Paula Cooper Gallery." *New York Times*, 4 October 1985, p. C24.

Smith, Roberta. "Group Show." *New York Times*, 17 February 1989, p. C34.

———. "More Women and Unknowns at the Whitney Biennial." *New York Times*, 28 April 1989, p. C32.

Stapen, Nancy. "Binational." *Art News*, December 1988, pp. 167-68.

Stern, William F. "Sculpture Inside/Outside." *Cité*, Spring/Summer 1989, pp. 20-21.

Vitale, Robert. "Robert Gober, Paula Cooper Gallery." *New Art Examiner*, January 1988, pp. 60-61.

JEFF KOONS

CATALOGS

A Decade of New Art. New York: Artists
Space, 1984.

Énergie New York. Lyon, France: ELAC
Centre d'Échanges, 1982.

A Fatal Attraction: Art and the Media.
Chicago: The Renaissance Society at the
University of Chicago, 1982.

Jeff Koons. Chicago: Museum of Contemporary Art, 1988.

The Los Angeles/New York Exchange. Los
Angeles: L.A. Contemporary Exhibitions,
1983.

*Mit dem Fernrohr durch die
Kunstgeschichte: Von Galilei zu den
gebrüdern Montgolfier.* Basel: Kunsthalle
Basel, 1989.

Objects, Structure, Artifice. Tampa:
University of South Florida, 1983.

ARTICLES

Albertazzi, Liliana. "Curators: Maria de
Corral." *Galeries,* February/March 1988,
p. 105.

Artner, Alan G. "New Media Show."
Chicago Tribune, Arts & Books, 9 May
1982, p. 17.

———— . "3 Sculptors Achieve Unsettling
Transformation of Everyday Objects."
Chicago Tribune, 11 May 1986, pp. 18-19.

Baker, Kenneth. "Review: Carnegie International, Carnegie Museum of Art." *Artforum,* March 1989, pp. 138-39.

Baker, Tom. "Modernism Without
Laughs." *Arena Magazine,* Summer/
Autumn 1987, p. 17.

Koons, Jeff. "'Baptism,' A Project for Artforum." *Artforum,* November 1987,
pp. 101-107.

Becker, Robert. "No Neo is Good Neo."
Blueprint, September 1987, p. 70.

Beyer, Lucie. *Flash Art,* February/March
1987, p. 111. Review.

Bonetti, David. "Under Full Sale: Koons
Gets Promoted." *The Boston Phoenix,*
6 January 1989.

Brenson, Michael. "Greed Plus Glitz,
With a Dollop of Innocence." *New York
Times,* 18 December 1988, p. B41.

———— . "International With Monument." *New York Times,* 10 October
1986, p. C32.

———— . "Shifting Image and Scale." *New
York Times,* 2 December 1988, p. C22.

Caley, Shaun. *Flash Art,* February/March
1987, p. 104. Review.

Cameron, Dan. "Pretty as a Product."
Arts Magazine, May 1986, p. 22.

Carlsen, Peter. "Jeff Koons." *Contemporanea,* September/October 1988, p. 38.

Casadio, Mariuccia. "Bickerton, Halley,
Koons e Vaisman: Le Premesse Teoriche
Dell'Oggetto Americano." *Vanity,*
July/August 1987, pp. 118-23.

Christov-Bakargiev, Carolyn. "New York
sepellisce il neoespressionismo e brinda al
ritorno di un arte 'certamente
americana.'" *Il Giornale Dell'Arte,* May
1987, pp. 99-100.

Chua, Lawrence. "Spotlight: Jeff Koons."
Flash Art, January/February 1989,
pp. 112-13.

"Collaborations: Jeff Koons & Martin
Kippenberger." *Parkett,* no. 19, 1989.

Cohen, Ronny "Energism: An Attitude."
Artforum, September 1980, pp. 16-23.

Collins, Tricia, and Milazzo, Richard.
"Benny 'Kid' Paret." *New Observations,*
March 1987, pp. 16-19.

———— . "Tropical Codes." *Kunstforum
International,* March/May 1986, pp.
308-37.

———— . "Tropical Codes: Jeff Koons."
Kunstforum International,
December/January 1988, pp. 84-87.

———— . "Whoever Sets Up Urinals
Shouldn't Wonder When They're Pissed
Into." *Wolkenkratzer,* January/February
1987, p. 86.

Cooke, Lynne. "New York, Sonnabend
Gallery, Jeff Koons." *Burlington
Magazine,* March 1989, pp. 246-47.

Coz, Meg. "Feeling Victimized? Then
Strike Back: Become an Artist." *Wall
Street Journal,* 13 February 1989, p. 1.

Craven, David. "Science Fiction and the
Future of Arts." *Arts Magazine,* May
1984, pp. 125-29.

Daniel, David. "Review: Jeff Koons at
Sonnabend." *Art & Antiques,* March
1989, p. 38.

Decter, Joshua. "New Ground." *Arts
Magazine,* December 1985, p. 123.

Deitch, Jeffrey. "Mythologies: Art and the
Market." *Artscribe International,* April/May
1986, pp. 22-26. Interviewed by Matthew
Collings.

Flacke, Christopher. "Held in Suspense."
Art & Antiques, Summer 1987, p. 25.

Flood, Richard. "Lighting." *Artforum,*
March 1981, pp. 69-70.

Nagy, Peter, moderator. "From Criticism
to Complicity." *Flash Art,* Summer 1986,
pp. 46-49.

Giachetti, Romano. "Di Loro Piace Quel
Piccolo Neo." *Epoca,* 5 May 1987,
pp. 50-55.

Gibson, Eric. "Decade in Review."
Sculpture, May/June 1989, pp. 21-23.

Glueck, Grace. "What Do You Call Art's
Newest Trend: 'NeoGeo'. . . Maybe." *New
York Times,* 6 July 1987, p. A13.

Gopnik, Adam. "The Art World." *The
New Yorker,* 23 May 1988, pp. 68-71.

———— . "The Art World: Lost and
Found." *Wall Street Journal,* 20 February
1989, pp. 107-11.

Graham-Dixon, Andrew. "Neo-Geo."
Vogue (British Edition), September 1987,
pp. 81-83.

Graw, Isabelle. "Atlantic Alliance."
Wolkenkratzer, January/February 1988,
pp. 36-43.

———. "Carnegie International." *Galeries*, December 1988/January 1989, pp. 76-78.

———. "Jeff Koons Kniefall Vor Dem Banalen." *Artis Das Aktuelle Kunstmagazin*, February 1989, pp. 24-27.

Gregorio, Magnani. "This Is Not Conceptual." *Flash Art*, March/April 1989, pp. 84-87.

Halley, Peter. "The Crisis in Geometry." *Arts Magazine*, Summer 1984, pp. 111-15.

———. "B.Z. and Michael Schwartz." *Galeries*, February/March 1989, pp. 118-29.

Heartney, Eleanor. "The 50th Carnegie: A Fin-de-siècle Brew of Pessimism and Hope." *New Art Examiner*, January 1989, pp. 26-29.

Hermes, Manfred. "Spotlight: The American Binational." *Flash Art*, January/February 1989, pp. 108-109.

Horn, Miriam. "The Avant-Garde: Moving into Middle America." *U.S. News & World Report*, 18 May 1987, pp. 68-69.

Indiana, Gary. "Art." *Village Voice*, 28 May 1985, p. 80.

———. "Paradigms of Dysfunction." *Village Voice*, 11 June 1985, p. 91.

———. "Jeff Koons at International With Monument." *Art In America*, November 1985, pp. 163-64.

———. "Formal Wares." *Village Voice*, 25 March 1986, p. 85.

———. "Time After Time." *Village Voice*, 25 March 1986, p. 85.

Jauault, Patrick. "Capc/musée d'art contemporain." *Art Press*, May 1988, p. 66.

"Jeff Koons and the Advertising of the Self." *Flash Art News*, January/Feburary 1989, p. 2.

Jones, Alan. "Jeff Koons." *Arts Magazine*, November 1983, p. 11.

———. "The Art of the Slam Dunk." *New York Talk*, May 1985, p. 47.

———. "The Kid." *New York Talk*, May 1986, p. 62.

———. "Paravision: An Interview With Tricia Collins and Richard Milazzo." *Galeries*, Summer 1986, p. 40.

———. "Thriller." *Contemporanea*, September/October 1988, p. 42.

———. "Jeff Koons: 'Et Qui Libre?'" *Galeries*, October/November 1986, pp. 94-97, 123.

Kleyn, Robert. "New Concepts." *Tema Celeste*, March 1987, pp. 59-61.

Knight, Christopher. "The L.A. Invasion of It." *Los Angeles Herald Examiner*, 10 August 1986, p. E11.

Kramer, Hilton. "Koons Show in the City Succeeds in Carrying Things to a New Low." *The New York Observer*, 19 December 1987, p. 1.

Lacayo, Richard. "Artist Jeff Koons Makes, and Earns, Giant Figures." *People Magazine*, 8 May 1989, p. 127.

Larson, Kay. "Love or Money." *New York Magazine*, 23 June 1986, pp. 65-66.

———. "Masters of Hype." *New York Magazine*, 10 November 1986, pp. 100-103.

Levin, Kim. "Admired Work." *Village Voice*, January 1986, p. 66.

———. "Art." *Village Voice*, 18 September 1985, p. 72.

———. "The Evil of Banality." *Village Voice*, 20 December 1988, p. 115.

———. "His Best Shot." *Village Voice*, 14 October, 1986, p. 96.

Liebman, Lisa. "Science Fiction." *Artforum*, December 1983, pp. 74-75.

McCracken, David. "Cuteness with an Edge in Jeff Koons' Work." *Chicago Tribune*, 16 December 1988, p. 43.

McGill, Douglas. "The Lower East Side's New Artist." *New York Times*, 3 June 1986, p. C13.

McKenna, Kristine. "The Art World is Ripe for Me." *Los Angeles Times*, "Calendar," 22 January 1989, p. 4.

Morgan, Stuart. "Big Fun: Four Reactions to the New Jeff Koons." *Artscribe International*, March/April 1989, pp. 46-49.

Muchnic, Susanne. "Commodity-Culture Art Rides Again." *Los Angeles Times*, 26 June 1986, Part V, p. 9.

Palmer, Laurie. *Artforum*, October 1988, p. 153. Review.

Perrault, John. "Functionaries." *Soho News*, 23 December 1981, p. 55.

Pinchbeck, Daniel. "Interview with Jeff Koons." *Splash*, 14 April 1989.

Pincus-Witten, Robert. "Entries: Concentrated Juice & Kitschy Kitschy Koons." *Arts Magazine*, February 1989, pp. 36-39.

———. "Entries: First Nights." *Arts Magazine*, January 1987, pp. 44-45.

———. "The Scene That Turned on a Dime." *Arts Magazine*, April 1986, pp. 20-21.

Plagens, Peter. "The Emperor's New Cherokee Limited 4x4." *Art in America*, June 1988, pp. 23-24.

Politi, Giancarlo. "Luxury and Desire, An Interview With Jeff Koons." *Flash Art*, Febuary/March 1987, pp. 71-76.

Power, Kevin. *Flash Art*, Febuary/March 1987, p. 113. Review.

Raynor, Vivien. "Art: Objects are Subject of (Damaged Goods)." *New York Times*, 18 July 1986, p. C21.

Relyea, Lane. "Hot Commodities." *L.A. Weekly*, 15-21 August 1986, p. 21.

Rubinstein, Meyer Raphael, and Wiener, Daniel. "Sites and Sights: Considerations on Walter DeMaria, Jeff Koons, and Tom Butter." *Arts Magazine*, March 1987, pp. 20-21.

Saltz, Jerry. "The Dark Side of the Rabbit: Notes on a Sculpture by Jeff Koons." *Arts Magazine*, February 1988, pp. 26-27.

Schwartman, Allan. "Corporate Culture: The Yippie-Yuppie Artist." *Manhattan Inc.*, December 1987, pp. 137-43.

Siegel, Jeanne. "The Artist Critic of the Eighties. Part One: Peter Halley and Stephen Westfall." *Arts Magazine*, September 1985, pp. 72-79.

Smith, Roberta. "Art: 4 Young East Villagers at Sonnabend Gallery." *New York Times*, 24 October 1986, p. C30.

——— . "Give Art a Chance." *Village Voice*, 1 January 1985, pp. 111-15.

——— . "Rituals of Consumption." *Art in America*, May 1988, pp. 164-71.

——— . "We Remember MOMA." *Village Voice*, 22 May 1984, p. 88.

Slesin, Suzanne. "Where Contemporary Art is the Decor." *New York Times*, 2 February 1988, p. C1.

Staniszewski, Mary Anne. "Conceptual Art of the '60s and the '70s Alienated the Viewer." *Flash Art*, November/December 1988, pp. 113-14.

——— . "Hot Commodities." *Manhattan Inc.*, June 1986, p. 159.

Taylor, Paul. "My Art Belongs to Dada." *Observer*, 6 September 1987, pp. 35-41.

——— . "Spotlight: Carnegie International." *Flash Art*, January/February 1989, p. 106.

Tillim, Sidney. "Ideology and Difference." *Arts Magazine*, March 1989, pp. 48-51.

Wallach, Amei. "The King of Art." *New York Newsday*, 1 December 1988, p. 4.

——— . "The New Art is SoHo Cool." *New York Newsday*, 26 October 1986, Part II, p. 3.

Wohlfert, Lee. "New York: Young Sculptors." *Town & Country*, September 1981, pp. 259-71.

ANNETTE LEMIEUX

CATALOGS

Annette Lemieux. New York: Josh Baer Gallery, 1989.

Annette Lemieux: The Appearance of Sound. Sarasota, Florida: The John and Mable Ringling Museum of Art, 1989.

The Beauty of Circumstance. New York: Josh Baer Gallery, 1987.

A Brave New World, A New Generation: Forty New York Artists. Copenhagen, Denmark: Udstillingsbygning Ved Charlottenborg; and Lund, Sweden: Lund Kunsthalle, 1985.

Hybrid Neutral. New York: Independent Curators Incorporated, 1988.

Jennifer Boland/Moira Dryer/Annette Lemieux. Philadelphia: Lawrence Oliver Gallery, 1987.

Media Post Media. New York: Scott Hanson Gallery, 1988.

The New Poverty. New York: John Gibson Gallery, 1987.

1987 Biennial Exhibition. New York: The Whitney Museum of American Art and W.W. Norton, 1987.

Photography on the Edge. Milwaukee: The Patrick and Beatrice Haggerty Museum of Art, 1988.

Photography of Invention: American Pictures of the 1980s. Washington, D.C., and Boston: National Museum of American Art and MIT Press, 1989.

The Pollock-Krasner Foundation, Inc., Annual Report, 1987-1988. New York: The Pollock-Krasner Foundation, 1988.

Prospect '89: Eine Internationale Austellung Aktueller Kunst. Frankfurt: Frankfurter Kunstverein and Schirn Kunsthalle, 1989.

Recent Tendencies in Black and White. New York: Sidney Janis Gallery, 1987.

Reprises de Vues. Geneva, Switzerland: Halle Sud, 1988.

Selected Prints and Multiples IV. New York: Brooke Alexander Editions, 1989.

INFAS: 7 Artists. Tokyo: INFAS, The Hanae Mori Foundation, 1989.

The Silent Baroque. Salzburg, Austria: Galerie Thaddeus Ropac, 1989.

Turn It Over. New York: White Columns, 1983.

Ultrasurd. Toronto: S.L. Simpson Gallery, 1986.

ARTICLES

Aletti, Vince. "The Return of the Hero." *Village Voice*, 1 March 1988.

"Annette Lemieux: Unbranded Cattle." *Kunstforum International*, April/May 1986, pp. 336-37.

Artner, Alan G. "What is New in Art." *Chicago Tribune*, 29 June 1986.

——— . "Lemieux Chooses Styles to Fit Concepts." *Chicago Tribune*, 27 May 1988, Sect. 7, p. 48.

Audiello, Massimo. "Guerra D'Artista." *Vanity*, no. 25, May/June 1987, pp. 114-19.

Bankowsky, Jack. "Annette Lemieux at Josh Baer Gallery." *Artforum*, Summer 1989, p. 139.

Bellavance, Leslie. "The Tragedy of Misconception." *Art Muscle*, November 1987/January 1988.

Biegler, Beth. "Deconstructing." *East Village Eye*, July 1985.

Bonetti, David. "Where's Boston? No Local Heroes at MFA/ICA Binational." *Boston Phoenix*, 23 September 1988.

Brenson, Michael. "Annette Lemieux." *New York Times*, 31 March 1989, p. C30.

Brooks, Rosetta. "Remembrance of Objects Past." *Artforum*, December 1986, pp. 68-69.

——— . "Space Fictions." *Flash Art*, December 1986/January 1989, pp. 78-80.

Cameron, Dan. "Report from the Front." *Arts Magazine*, March 1986, p. 88.

——— . "Post-Feminism." *Flash Art*, February/March 1987, pp. 80-83.

——— . "The Whitney Biennial." *Flash Art*, Summer 1987, pp. 86-87.

——— . "Opening Salvos Part I." *Arts Magazine*, December 1987.

Collins, Tricia, and Milazzo, Richard. "Neutral Trends." *East Village Eye*, October 1985.

——— . "Tropical Codes." *Kunstforum International*, December 1987/January 1988, pp. 104-107.

——— . "Time After Time." *Halle Sud* (Geneva), no. 17, Première Trimestre 1988.

Cottingham, Laura. "The Feminine De-Mystique." *Flash Art*, Summer 1989.

Decter, Joshua. "Annette Lemieux." *Arts Magazine*, Summer 1989.

"Downtown Style." *Vogue*, September 1988.

Edwards, Lee. "The Labor of Psyche." *Aperture*, Spring 1988, p. 53.

Gimelson, Deborah. "Ammann For All Seasons." *Art & Auction*, November 1987.

Handy, Ellen. "Group Show." *Arts Magazine*, September 1986.

Helfland, G. "Objects of Desire." *Artweek*, 29 October 1988, p. 4.

Indiana, Gary. "Talking Back." *Village Voice*, 11 February 1986.

——— . "Formal Wares." *Village Voice*, 25 March 1986.

——— . "Annette Lemieux at Cash/Newhouse." *Art in America* July 1986, p. 119.

——— . "Enclosed by System." *Village Voice*, 9 December 1986.

——— . "Future Perfect." *Village Voice*, 10 March 1987.

——— . "Another Review of the Whitney." *Village Voice*, 28 April 1987.

Jones, Nancy. "Poetry in Paint." *New York Woman*, March 1989, p. 58.

Jones, Ronald. "Group Show at Brooke Alexander." *Artscribe International*, November/December 1986, p. 77.

——— . "Every Future Has A Price." *ZG*, no. 15, 1988, pp. 25-27.

Kent, Sarah. "New Reviews." *Time Out*, March 1988.

Kimmelman, Michael. "Touring Show of Soviet and American Artists." *New York Times*, 16 May 1989, p. C15.

Koether, Jutta. "What's on the Run Stays." *Parkett*, no. 16, 1988.

Leigh, Christian. "Annette Lemieux, Wadsworth Atheneum." *Artforum*, September 1988, p. 145.

——— . "Art on the Verge of a Nervous Breakdown." *Contemporanea*, January 1989, p. 101.

——— . "Into the Blue." *Art & Auction*, May 1989, p. 264.

Lemieux, Annette. "Sonnet: Project for Artscribe." *Artscribe International*, Summer 1987, pp. 42-43.

Levin, Kim. "Art: The Antique Future." *Village Voice*, 10 March 1987.

——— . "Art: Annette Lemieux." *Village Voice*, 5 May 1987.

——— . "Art: Fake." *Village Voice*, 30 June 1987.

——— . "Modern Sleep." *Village Voice*, 11 November 1987.

——— . "Annette Lemieux." *Village Voice*, 11 April 1989.

Linker, Kate. "Eluding Definition." *Artforum*, December 1984, pp. 61-67.

Lovelace, Carey. "The Whitney Gets It Right...Almost." *New Art Examiner*, Summer 1987.

McCoy, Pat. "of Ever-Ever Land I speak." *Artscribe International*, January/February 1988.

Messler, Norbert. "And Meager Magnetism." *Artforum*, March 1989, p. 67.

Miller, John. "Subtext." *Artscribe International*, November/December 1987, p. 74.

——— . "Media Post Media." *Artscribe International*, May 1988, pp. 77-78.

Mohoney, Robert. "Time After Time." *Arts Magazine*, March 1986.

Newhall, Edith. "'Blow Ups' Photo Album." *New York*, 12 December 1988.

Papa, Sania. "Collections: Dakis Joannou." *Galeries*, October/November 1988, p. 154.

Perl, Jed. "Artburn: The State of the Art World in the '80s." *Vogue*, May 1987, p. 368.

Pincus-Witten, Robert. "Entries: Annette Lemieux, An Obsession With Stylistics: Painter's Guilt." *Arts Magazine*, September 1988, pp. 32-37.

Plagens, Peter. "Under Western Eyes." *Art in America*, January 1989, p. 41.

Raynor, Vivien. *New York Times*, 12 September 1986, p. C21. Review.

Rimanelli, David. "Pre-Pop/Post-Appropriation." *Artforum*, May 1989.

Robinson, William. "New New York." *New Art Examiner*, June 1986, p. 54.

Robinson, Walter. "Odd Lots." *East Village Eye*, December 1984.

Rubey, Dan. "The Antique Future." *Art News*, October 1987.

Salvioni, Daniela. "Spotlight: Annette Lemieux." *Flash Art*, Summer 1987, p. 99.

Schwabsky, Barry. "Diversion, Oblivion and the Pursuit of New Objects: Reflections on Another Biennial." *Arts Magazine*, Summer 1987, pp. 78-80.

Schwendenwein, Jude. *Art New England*, September 1988, p. 23.

——— . "Conceptual Chameleon." *Elle*, April 1989, p. 192.

———— . "Pre-Pop/Post-Appropriation."
Tema Celeste, Summer 1989.
Siegel, Jeanne. "It's a Wonderful Life, Or
Is It?" *Arts Magazine*, January 1987,
pp. 78-81.
Smith, Roberta. "Art: Annette Lemieux
in Two Mixed Media Shows." *New York
Times*, 17 April 1987, p. C26.
———— . "Sculpture, The Works of Five
Women." *New York Times*, 2 October
1987, p. C26.

———— . "Art: 'Media Post Media,' A
show of 19 Women." *New York Times*, 15
January 1988, p. C24.
———— . "Galleries Paint a Brighter
Picture for Women." *New York Times*, 14
April 1989, p. C21.
Spector, Nancy. "Group Exhibition, Pat
Hearn." *Artscribe International*,
January/February 1988, pp. 69-70.
Staniszewski, Mary Anne. "Corporate
Culture—Gallery Guide." *Manhattan
Inc.*, April 1987, p. 176.
Stapen, Nancy. "Shock Value—Is Proper
Boston Ready For 'The Binational'
Exhibit?" *Boston Herald*, 23 September
1988.

Taylor, Robert. "The Binational Running
on Empty." *Boston Sunday Globe*, 25
September 1988, p. 89.
Warren, Ron. "57 Between A & D." *Arts
Magazine*, April 1985, p. 38.
Wilson, William. *Los Angeles Times*,
1 April 1988.
Woodruff, Mark. "The Antique Future:
Articulating the Void." *New Art Examiner*,
June 1987, pp. 36-37.

JUAN MUÑOZ

CATALOGS

Aperto 86: Cuatro Artistas Españoles.
Venice: Biennale di Venezia, 1986
*Ateliers Internationaux des Pays de la
Loire.* Paris: Fondation nationale des arts
graphiques et plastiques, 1986.
*C. Dighgans, L. Dujourie, M. Dumas, L.
Foxcroft . . . J. Muñoz, et al.* Eindhoven:
Stedelijk Van Abbemuseum, 1985.
Chambres d'Amis. Gent: Museum van
Hedendaagse Kunst, 1986.
5th Salon de los 16. Madrid: Museo
Español de Arte Contemporáneo, 1985.
La Imagen del Animal. Madrid: Caja del
Monte, 1983.
Juan Muñoz. Bordeaux: capc Musée d'art
contemporain, 1987.
Juan Muñoz, Ultimos Trabajos. Madrid:
Galería Fernando Vijande, 1984.

Lili Dujourie/Juan Muñoz. Abbaye de
Fontevraud: FRAC des Pays de La Loire,
1987.
*1981-1986. Pintores y Escultores
Españoles.* Madrid: Fundación Caja de
Pensiones, 1986.
Seis Españoles en Madrid. Madrid:
Galería Fernando Vijande, 1983.

ARTICLES

Melo, A. "Some Things Cannot be Said
Any Other Way." *Artforum*, May 1989,
pp. 119-21.
Brea, J. L. "Juan Muñoz—The System of
Objects." *Flash Art*, January/February
1988, pp. 88-89.

PUBLICATIONS BY THE ARTIST

"The best sculpture is a toy horse."
Domus, March 1985.

"Correspondencias." *5 Arquitectos/5
Escultores.* Madrid: Palacio de la Alhajas,
1983.
"Desde...a..." *Figura*, Spring 1986.
"El hijo major de Laooconte." Bern:
Kunstmuseum Bern, 1986.
"La imagen prohibida o el juego de la
Rayuela." *Code*, 1987.
"De la luminosa opacidad de los signos."
Figura, Autumn 1986.
"Los Primeros—Los Últimos." *La Im-
agen del Animal.* Madrid: Casa del
Monte, 1983.
"Nada es tan opaco como un espejo."
Sur Express, April/May 1987.
"La palabra como escultura." *Figura*,
Winter 1985.
"Richard Long: de la precisión en las
distancias." *Richard Long.* Madrid:
Palacio de Cristal, 1986.

JULIAN OPIE

CATALOGS

Art and Language, Julian Opie. London:
Lisson Gallery, 1985.
De Sculptura—Junge Bildhauer 1986.
Vienna: Wiener Festwochen, 1986.

Julian Opie: Drawings 1982-1985. London:
Institute of Contemporary Art, 1985.
Il Progetto Domestico. Milan: XVII Trien-
nale di Milano, 1986.
Julian Opie. Cologne: Kölnischer
Kunstverein, 1984.

*Three British Sculptors: Richard Deacon,
Julian Opie, Richard Wentworth.*
Jerusalem: The Israel Museum, 1985.

ARTICLES

Allthorpe-Guyton, Marjorie. "Julian Opie, Lisson Gallery." *Flash Art*, February/March 1987, p. 109.

Andrae, Christopher. "Having a Fling with History." *Christian Science Monitor*, 29 June 1985.

Baker, Kenneth. "Julian Opie." *Louisiana Revy*, 2 March 1987.

——. *San Francisco Chronicle*, June 1987.

Baker, Tom. "House of Fun." *The Face*, April 1988.

Batchelor, David. "Julian Opie, Lisson." *Artscribe International*, March/April 1987, pp. 70-71.

Berryman, Larry. "Julian Opie, Lisson Gallery." *Arts Review*, December 1986, p. 670.

Cooke, Lynne. "Julian Opie and Simon Linke: Two Young British Artists Speak about Their Work and Their Context Internationally." *Flash Art*, April 1987, pp. 37-39.

——. *Art International*, Summer 1988, pp. 50-51. Review.

Cork, Richard. "In a Hurry." *The Listener*, 2 May 1985.

Kent, Sarah. *Time Out*, 18-24 April 1985.

——. *Art in America*, June 1988, p. 171. Review.

Lovely, David. "Casting an Eye, Cornerhouse." *Artscribe International*, May 1987, pp. 71-72.

Newman, Michael. "La Double Ironie de Julian Opie." *Art Press*, February 1984, pp. 34-35.

Paul, Diane. "The Nine Lives of Discredited Data." *The Sciences*, May/June 1987.

Pohlen, Annelie. "Julian Opie and Tony Cragg." *Kunstforum International*, September/October 1984, p. 194.

Shone, Richard. *Burlington Magazine*, April 1988, p. 308. Review.

Thomas, Mona. "Intimes Gentillesses de l'homme Julian Opie." *Beaux Arts Magazine*, May 1985.

Vaizey, Marina. "Nurturing Talent in a Narrow Frame." *Sunday Times* (London), 13 March 1988.

HAIM STEINBACH

CATALOGS

Arts and Leisure. New York: The Kitchen, 1986.

Haim Steinbach: Recent Works. Bordeaux: capc, Musée d'art contemporain, 1988.

Infotainment. New York: J Berg Press, 1985.

Innovations in Sculpture 1985-88. Ridgefield: The Aldrich Museum of Contemporary Art, 1988.

Les courtiers du désir. Paris: Centre Georges Pompidou, 1987.

New York Now. Phoenix: Phoenix Art Museum, 1979.

Reconstruct. New York: John Gibson Gallery, 1987.

ReDefining the Object. Dayton: University Art Galleries, Wright State University, 1988.

Repetition. New York: Hirschl & Adler Modern, 1989.

Schlaf der Vernunft. Kassel: Museum Fridericianum, 1988.

ARTICLES

Arnaudet, Didier. "Haim Steinbach: C.A.P.C., Bordeaux." *Contemporanea*, April 1989.

"Artists Talk." *Flash Art News*, November/December 1988.

Avgikos, Jan. "The Binational: ICA Boston." *Artscribe International*, Summer 1989.

Ball, Edward. "The Beautiful Language of My Century." *Arts Magazine*, January 1989, p. 70.

Beith, Reinhard. "Gartenschlauch, Scherzartikel und Staubsauger." *Die Welt*, March 1988.

Bochner, Mel. "Ileana Sonnabend." *Galeries*, June/July 1988.

Celant, Germano. "Haim Steinbach's Wild, Wild West." *Artforum*, December 1987, pp. 75-79.

Christov-Bakargiev, Carolyn. "Haim Steinbach, Staging the Illusion of Fake." *Flash Art*, March/April 1988, p. 104.

Cornand, Brigitte. "Inexpressionniste ou Déconstructioniste." *Actuel*, April 1989.

Cotter, Holland. "Haim Steinbach: Shelf Life." *Art in America*, May 1988, pp. 156-63.

Curtis, Cathy. *Los Angeles Times*, 9 June 1989. Review.

Czoppan, Gabi. "Fussballelf und Eishockeypuck, Das Skulpturenprojekt Durr." *Münchner Stadtzeitung*, May 1988. p. 152.

——. "Gallerie, New York Im Auge." *Münchner Stadtzeitung*, June 1988.

Deitch, Jeffrey. "Geometrie Culturali." *Flash Art* (Italy), March/April 1988, pp. 50-52.

Dittmar, Peter. "Coldfish mit Psychose." *Die Welt*, February 1988, p. 19.

Dreher, Thomas. "New York in View, München, Kunstverein." *Artefactum*, September/October 1988.

Faust, Wolfgang Max. "Now New York New." *Wolkenkratzer*, January 1988.

Graw, Isabelle. "The Sleep of Reason." *Flash Art*, Summer 1988, pp. 139-40.

Jones, Ronald. "Hover Culture." *Artscribe International*, Summer 1988, pp. 46-61.

Karcher, Eva. "Auf dem Vormarsch." *Münchner Theaterzeitung*, March 1988, p. 85.

Leigh, Christian. "Art on the Verge of a Nervous Breakdown." *Contemporanea*, January/February 1989.

———. "Haim Steinbach at Jay Gorney Modern Art." *Artforum*, October 1988, pp. 143-44.

Marter, Joan. "The World Financial Center: 'The New Urban Landscape.'" *Arts Magazine*, March 1989.

Miller, John. "The Consumption of Everyday Life." *Artscribe International*, January/February 1988, pp. 46-52.

Morgan, Robert. "Haim Steinbach at Jay Gorney Modern Art." *Flash Art*, October 1988, pp. 128-29.

———. "The Spectrum of Object-Representation." *Arts Magazine*, October 1988, pp. 78-80.

Morgan, Stuart. "School of Athens." *Artscribe International*, March/April 1988.

Nemeczek, Alfred. "Geduldig den Augenaufschlag abwarten." *Art*, April 1988, p. 30.

Nickas, Robert. "Shopping with Haim Steinbach." *Flash Art*, October 1987, p. 105.

Perreault, John. "Through a Glass Darkly." *Artforum*, March 1989.

Schwarze, Dirk. "Das Kasseler Museum Fridericianum als Kunsthalle, Eine zu stille Ausstellung." *HNA Kultur*, April 1988.

———. "'Schlaf der Vernunft,' im Kasseler Museum Fridericianum, Zwischen den Stilen." *HNA Kultur*, March 1988.

Schwartzmann, Allan. "Corporate Trophies." *Art in America*, February 1989, pp. 35-43.

Siegel, Jeanne. "Suits, Suitcases and Other Look-Alikes." *Arts Magazine*, April 1989, p. 71.

Smith, Roberta. "Haim Steinbach at Jay Gorney Modern Art." *New York Times*, 3 June 1988, p. C25.

———. "A Wide Ranging Spread of Artists and Installations." *New York Times*, 4 November 1988, p. C24.

Steinbach, Haim. "The Joy of Tapping Our Feet." *Parkett*, November 1988, pp. 16-21.

Taylor, Paul. "Haim Steinbach: An Easygoing Aesthetic That Appeals to the Flaneur in Many of Us." *Flash Art*, May/June 1989, pp. 133-34.

———. "Object Lessons." *House and Garden*, October 1988.

NEWPORT HARBOR ART MUSEUM

S T A F F

ADMINISTRATION
Karen Ables, *Accountant*
Evan Ballinger, *Accounting Assistant*
Christopher Cyga, *Accounting Assistant*
Ursula R. Cyga, *Admissions and Membership Officer*
Robert Leslie, *Admissions Assistant*
Carol Lincoln, *Chief Accountant*
Andy Meginnis, *Systems Administrator*
Claire Pardue, *Executive Secretary*
Jane Piasecki, *Associate Director*
Carolyn Sellers, *Receptionist*

DEVELOPMENT
Eunice Cluck, *Development and Campaign Assistant*
Kathleen D. Costello, *Associate Director of Development*
Maxine Gaiber, *Public Relations Officer*
Dee Lynn, *Public Relations and Membership Assistant*
Margaret O'Malley, *Membership Coordinator*
Charles P. Ries, *Capital Campaign Director*
Aubrey Robin, *Development Assistant*
Margie M. Shackelford, *Director of Development*

EDUCATION
Ellen Breitman, *Director of Education*
Kathy McFarlane, *Education Assistant*
Karin Schnell, *Assistant Director of Education*

EXHIBITIONS
Lucinda Barnes, *Associate Curator*
Paula Chavez, *Registration Intern*
Lorraine Dukes *Assistant to the Chief Curator*
Marilu Knode, *Assistant Curator*
Paul Schimmel, *Chief Curator*
Betsy Severance, *Registrar*

MUSEUM STORE
Kirin Anderson, *Store Assistant*
Patricia Caspary, *Store Manager*

OPERATIONS
Chris Gallup, *Preparator*
Dan Goodsell, *Preparator*
Brian Gray, *Exhibition Designer*
Lynn Kubasek, *Preparator*
Ginny Lee, *Preparator*
Matt Leslie, *Chief of Security*
Richard Tellinghuisen, *Director of Operations*
Robert G. Zingg, *Preparator*

PUBLICATIONS
Sue Henger, *Museum Editor*
Sandy O'Mara, *Graphic Designer*

SCULPTURE GARDEN CAFE
Marilyn Kaun, *Cafe Manager*

PHOTO CREDITS

Abbaye Royal, Fontevraud, France, p. 128

Courtesy Josh Baer Gallery, New York, p. 105, 107,
   109, 115, 117

Courtesy Galerie Jean Bernier, Athens, p. 73

Courtesy capc Musée d'art contemporain,
   Bordeaux, p. 119

Geoffrey Clements, New York, p. 71, 77

Courtesy Galerie Joost Declercq, Gent, p. 133

James Dee, New York, p. 66, 67, 70 (right), 76, 78,
   79, 80 (top), 81

Frederic Delpech, p. 166, 167

Volker Döhne, Krefeld, p. 50, 54, 60, 61

Scott Firth, London, p. 39, 40

Courtesy Galerie Konrad Fischer, Düsseldorf,
   p. 131, 132

Hansen/Mayer, Boston, p. 74, 75

Courtesy Ydessa Hendeles, Toronto, p. 48

Bill Jacobson, New York, p. 116

Courtesy Johnen & Schöttle, Cologne, p. 51-53, 55, 65

Courtesy Kunsthalle Basel, p. 62, 63

Courtesy Lisson Gallery, London, p. 32, 47, 138-140

David Lubarsky, New York, p. 20, 154-165, 168, 169

Courtesy Galerie Paul Maenz, Cologne, p. 143

Andrew Moore, New York, p. 69, 70 (left)

Susan Ormerod, London, p. 34-37, 41-46, 144-153

Douglas M. Parker Studio, Los Angeles, p. 112

Galería Marga Paz, Madrid, p. 120, 123, 127, 130

Thomas Ruff, Düsseldorf, p. 56-59

Ken Schles, p. 111

Wilhelm Schürmann, Herzogenrath, Courtesy
   Galerie Gisela Capitain, p. 80 (bottom)

Fred Scruton, New York, p. 83-85, 87-99

Courtesy Sonnabend Gallery, New York, p. 86

Courtesy Monika Sprüth Gallery, Cologne, p. 14

J. P. Tessore, p. 125

Michael Tropea, Chicago, p. 114

Henni Van Beek, Amsterdam, p. 64

Courtesy Wadsworth Atheneum, p. 106

James Welling, New York, p. 101

Larry Wheelock, p. 113

Ellen Page Wilson, p. 103

Gareth Winters, London, p. 31, 33, 118, 134, 135,
   137, 141

Piet Ysable, p. 129